BEST OF BRITISH FISH

IN ASSOCIATION WITH
THE ROYAL NATIONAL MISSION
TO DEEP SEA FISHERMEN

BEST OF BRITISH
FISH

compiled by HATTIE ELLIS
AND CAMILLA SACCHI
introduction and profiles by
HATTIE ELLIS

MITCHELL BEAZLEY

FOREWORD

When we think about the sea, our thoughts are mostly of calm waters and idyllic sunny beaches, but the fact is that it is the most powerful force on our planet and, when it rages, can destroy most things in its path. There are people who have no choice but to work on the ocean in all weathers — our fishermen. Every single day, the lives of these 14,000 men are at risk. Fishing is the most dangerous industry in the UK today. Each month three boats are lost at sea and 10 fishermen are killed or seriously injured. Overnight, families lose their loved ones and breadwinners, and tiny communities are devastated. There is one charity there to help them through their tragedy — The Fishermen's Mission.

Serious injury is a routine hazard of working in the fishing industry and, apart from the pain, it can also mean the loss of a vital livelihood. When we buy our fish we don't consider how hard it is to get it to us. The Royal National Mission to Deep Sea Fishermen wants us to understand its key message. The real cost of fish isn't measured in pounds and pence, but in men's lives and families' losses. The charity covers the whole coastline. It plays a key role in rescue operations and guides families through their trauma. Every single one of us owes it to Britain's fishing communities to think long and hard about just how much we owe the men who risk their lives at sea.

Rick Stein

First published in Great Britain in 2005 by Mitchell Beazley, an imprint of Octopus Publishing Group Limited,
2–4 Heron Quays, London E14 4JP.
Design and layout © Octopus Publishing Group Ltd 2005
Introduction & profiles © Hattie Ellis 2005

A CIP catalogue record for this book is available from the British Library.
ISBN 1 84000 999 3

Concept: Simon Impey of ebb and flow
Words: Hattie Ellis
Fishing consultant: Camilla Sacchi
Commissioning editor: Rebecca Spry
Executive art editor: Yasia Williams
Design: Lawrence Morton
Editor: Diona Gregory
Photography: Peter Cassidy (food)
       & Simon Impey (location) with
       additional locations by Camilla Sacchi
Location photographic assistant: Ersoy Emin
Home economy and styling: Linda Tubby
Production: Gary Hayes
Index: John Noble

CONTENTS

THE FISHERMEN'S MISSION

The Fishermen's Mission has been supporting British fishermen and their families for almost 125 years. The Mission was founded in 1881, in the year when a great storm claimed the lives of 130 fishermen off Eyemouth, many of whom were killed on the shore within sight of their families. It is a Christian society with a no-nonsense approach to providing pastoral care and practical help to fishermen and their families, regardless of their race or creed.

The Mission is represented in more than 70 fishing ports in Britain, and in all the major ports it runs a centre that provides low-cost accommodation, catering and other facilities for fishermen and their wives and children. In remote fishing communities the Mission building is often a focal point and centre of activity for the whole village.

At the core of the Mission's work are the port staff, affectionately known as 'the Mission men'. Crossing all religious divides, the Mission man or woman is there to provide pastoral care and practical support to fishermen and their families in times of tragedy, illness or grief. Fishing is inherently dangerous, as it involves the handling of very heavy gear on slippery decks in a heaving vessel. Working long hours, with little rest, often in appalling weather conditions, far from land, fishermen face the daily reality that their vessel may be severely damaged or overwhelmed by the sea. Despite rigorous safety precautions on board, the sea is an unforgiving environment.

Thus, sadly, fishing remains by far the UK's most dangerous industry, with the risk of accident or death being more than 50 times greater than the average peacetime occupation. Almost 30 UK fishing boats sink each year, and the Mission is there to care for those whose lives are shattered by bereavement or whose breadwinner has been seriously injured. This help can continue for years, with the Mission keeping in touch with the family and delivering financial assistance to wives or partners and children.

Thank you to all the chefs, fishermen, fishmongers and supporters who have contributed to Best of British Fish. Thanks to their help, this book celebrates the UK's fishermen and the work of the Royal National Mission within our fishing communities. As you enjoy your fish, please give thought to those who have caught it.

CAPTAIN DAN CONLEY, OBE, RN,
CHIEF EXECUTIVE OF THE FISHERMEN'S MISSION

FOR THE FISHERMEN AND THE MISSION MEN OF THE UK

INTRODUCTION

Everybody has some salt in their blood. As well as the childhood pleasures of beach cricket and vanilla ice-creams, we are drawn to windswept walks by the sea to put life into perspective against the elements. In the same way, the salty business of fishing has washed into our imaginations and animates the day-to-day life of the edge of our islands. In a working port such as Newlyn in Cornwall, every stone, every rope, every raucous seagull's cry leads back to the harbour, with its constant hum of boat engines and its cats slinking around looking for fish bones. In nearby Mousehole, the retired fishermen of a bygone age used to take their constitutional walks along the seafront, turning round after they'd done the length of a ship's deck.

While we have salt in our blood, most of us only stand on the edge of the sea, and the most common way that we connect with it, in a practical sense, is through eating fish. The fisherman has traditionally been a tough but romantic figure, who goes between us and the dark, unknown waters and brings back dinner. He still goes out to sea with little protection and works with machinery that would be dangerous even without the constantly heaving, slippery sway of the sea. There are about 6,700 boats in the British fishing fleet, mostly family-owned, and for those who go out in them, fishing is still the most dangerous civilian work in the world. Death is part of the life of fishermen, a melancholy undertow which these communities have to live with.

Yet in these environmentally uncertain times, there are fears for the sea and its fish, for the biodiversity and cleanness of the marine environment, but not always, it seems, for the fishermen.

Though the status of fish as a healthy food has risen dramatically, there continues to be a drastic decline in the fisherman's income that has left fishing

'IT IS IMPORTANT WE FOSTER A LOVE OF FISH

families around the coast without boats. Over the past few years the number of boats has fallen by more than a third because fishermen have been paid to scrap their boats (a process known as 'decommissioning'), in an attempt to conserve declining fish stocks. In Scotland, the white fish fleet has declined by 62 per cent since 2000. For the fisherman, a boat is a way of life, not merely a place of work, and such a loss is devastating both to the man and the community.

Fishermen often argue that there are more effective methods of control to sustain fish stocks and secure the future of their industry. There are emerging theories about how to rebuild and maintain the numbers of fish, for example, by leaving some areas unfished at certain times of the year ('closed areas'), by altering fishing gear, and by getting fishermen, who are innately competitive, to ensure that their particular region is sustainably fished by everyone.

As the serious issues about conserving fish stocks are discussed and acted upon, this should not mean that we drop this special food from our diets, or make us lose sight of the people who catch it. For the consumer, a positive approach is to treat fish with the respect it deserves, eating a wider variety to take the pressure off endangered stocks, and paying more for it if necessary.

It is important that we foster a love of fish because the problems of fishing have partly arisen through a lack of engagement. In countries such as Iceland, people have found ways to promote sustainable fisheries because those ashore want to have a good, long-lasting supply of high-quality seafood. (Thirty per cent of the cod on sale in Britain comes from Iceland; under five per cent comes from the North Sea.)

A collage of recipes follows, collected from some of the people who care most about seafood and who bring it from the sea to our plates. They have donated their

BECAUSE PROBLEMS HAVE PARTLY ARISEN THROUGH LACK OF ENGAGEMENT.'

recipes in aid of The Fishermen's Mission, the national charity that looks after fishermen, and the families of fishermen, who have died or been injured at sea.

Those who handle fish most often — fishermen, fishmongers, chefs, home cooks — never lose a sense of excitement about British seafood. This starts with its sheer beauty. To stand in front of a good fishmonger's slab is to have the pick of nature's colours, forms and textures. You even welcome a bit of a queue in a fishmonger's so there is time to pick out what looks best. It is a privilege to eat.

Fish-folk never lose the sense of being lucky to have this food on their plate because of the risks of fishing and its unpredictability. In the markets and fish shops, availability and price vary according to time, tide, luck, risk and weather. A particular species can rise and fall steeply in cost from week to week according to catch and demand: an individual fisherman might catch nothing for weeks because of high winds; there may be a big haul of fine fish, bringing the price down; or the traders in a fish market may cluster around a fine landing of one species, kept in good condition and gleaming fresh from the sea, or 'stiff-alive' as the saying goes.

Everyone in the fish food chain has their favourite species and their tips for the underrated ones. There are recipes for both sorts in this book. For many, turbot is one of the most delicious fish. Its gelatinous bones make for beautifully textured flesh and sauces. Sea bass is another darling of the restaurant table, and fishermen admire its fighting spirit, catching the best by line as it swims in fierce tidal races. Other fishermen think John Dory 'the finest fish that swims'. The wild salmon, now rare, has regained its status as the prince of fish. Many of our shellfish, such as oysters, mussels and lobsters, are acclaimed for their sweet succulence. Dover sole keeps its flavour for longer than other flat fish, and its firm fillets retain

'FISH-FOLK NEVER LOSE THE SENSE OF BEING LUCKY TO HAVE THIS FOOD ON THEIR PLATES.'

their high status, and price — yet find other flat fish that have been freshly landed, such as a plump plaice, and you'll still get a good meal for a fraction of the price.

The price of fish is also influenced by fashion and popularity. Monkfish used to be thrown away, or used as fake scampi; now it fetches a premium because of its firm texture and lack of bones. If you ask fishmongers, fishermen and fish chefs for their tips for the most underrated fish, they often have a few candidates. However, they will confess, when pushed, that there is always a 'but' to their enthusiasm that explains the fish's relatively low price-tag. Yet any snags are often easily overcome with a bit of knowledge and practise in the shop and kitchen and on the plate, reinforcing the fact that fish, while not difficult to cook, requires a little attention, as befits what is still, for the most part, a special, wild food.

So it is that grey mullet is recommended by many — but only if it has been caught in open waters; not if it has fed in the harbour and tastes murky. Some people love dabs, with their tender pearly flesh, but they are small and therefore a touch fiddly. Ling is much praised, but it often swims on rocky ground and so may have to be line-caught (a selective fishing method that does not damage the seabed), which means it is harder to find on the fishmonger's slab. Huss is another overlooked fish, but you may have to change its name to sell it; one restaurateur called it vitello di mare (veal of the sea), and it flew off the menu.

Crustacean dealers can't understand why spider crabs are so underrated when they have such a good flavour, but you have to be prepared to linger over your meal, winning sweet shards of flesh from their long legs. Other species take their time in the cooking. Matt Tebbutt of The Foxhunter Inn near Abergavenny, one of the emerging gastropubs popularizing different kinds of fish, loves the bargain

'IN THE MARKETS AND SHOPS, AVAILABILITY AND PRICE VARY ACCORDING

TO TIME, TIDE, LUCK, RISK AND WEATHER.'

THE PRICE OF A PARTICULAR SPECIES of fish
can rise and fall steeply according to
catch and demand.

'OUR LOVE OF SEAFOOD IS OFTEN FED BY RESTAURANT MEALS ON HOLIDAY IN, SAY, SPAIN, WHERE WE EAT WHAT MAY HAVE BEEN EXPORTED FROM BRITAIN.'

cephalopod, the octopus, and says all you need to do is cook it slowly with garlic. He has persisted in keeping it on his menu and, gradually, it's getting a following.

Pollack is heading up the popularity stakes, as it can be used instead of cod. A couple of chefs told me how to salt pollack, cod and other similar fish for 20 minutes or so, then wash off the salt, so the fish's texture will be much improved.

As a nation, we've sadly lost sight of one of the fish that used to be a staple and founded the fortunes of many of our main fishing ports: herring. Like most oily fish, it deteriorates more rapidly – and rancidly – than other fish once caught. But catch a 'silver darling' at its best, then coat in oatmeal, fry and serve it simply with potatoes, and you'll never forget it.

The irridescent mackerel is one of the most beautiful fish as well as one of the cheapest. It is easily the most commonly landed fish from British waters: almost double the amount of the next most landed, the herring. We eat little of either fresh, and export many of our prime fish to Spain and other European countries. The irony is that our love of seafood is often fed by restaurant meals on holiday in, say, Spain, where we unknowingly eat what may have been exported from Britain.

This book has recipes and tips on how to enjoy what, by happy geographical circumstance, surrounds our shores. They come from people who couldn't be closer to their ingredients. There are the garlic prawns a Shetland skipper cooks for his Christmas Day starter; a superbly simple recipe from a cook in a Cornish fishing cove using the area's mixed catch, and a squid recipe that a Brighton fisherman puts in his slow cooker ready for supper when he gets home from the sea. From fishmongers come recipes for potted shrimps and a version of Cullen skink that makes use of what's lying around on the slab. From a book by a

'EVERY PERSON IN THIS BOOK
KNOWS THEIR INGREDIENTS
FROM SEA TO PLATE.'

coastguard-turned-writer and artist in the Hebrides there are tips on how to catch and cook razor clams by whisking them through a pan. Often it is the simple ways with seafood that make you feel hungriest.

Many chefs and food writers find fish the most fascinating ingredient of all and use all their technique and knowledge on it without losing sight of its essential freshness. Together, the recipes they have given show the versatility of seafood: using it raw, in soups, grilled, salt-baked, tossed with pasta, poached in oil, curried, stir-fried, deep-fried, however and whatever, sauced and sourced, with love and care.

Some of the contributors to Best of British Fish, such as Hugh Fearnley-Whittingstall and Marco Pierre White, are themselves keen fishermen. Mitchell Tonks and Rowley Leigh are chefs with fish shops. Every person in this book knows their ingredients from sea to plate, whether through working with suppliers, cooking with fish day-in, day-out, or by coming from a family where they have fished for generations.

We are lucky enough to be able to include classic recipes by such specialist fish restaurants as The Riverside in West Bay in Dorset, where they can get fish deliveries three times a day (and where they are not afraid to include a serious note about the importance of conservation on the menu). Also in the South-West, Tina and Tony Bricknell-Webb, at Percy's in Devon, are so fanatical about the quality of their fish that they buy direct from the small, top-notch Looe market, and in St Ives, Grant Nethercott at Alba won the accolade of AA Seafood Restaurant of the Year, thanks to his skills and the quality of his supplies. Part of the flavour of fresh fish – fading with age – comes from components in the flesh that are literally part

of the sea. After eating truly fresh fish in places such as these for a while, you start to require this particular taste, as fleeting and refreshing as a sea breeze.

In Scotland, a chef such as Shirley Spear at The Three Chimneys on the Isle of Skye can tell what she's going to be cooking that day by looking out of the window and phoning the skipper's mobile as he comes in to land. Alan Craigie at The Creel on South Ronaldsay in Orkney gets fish that are actually too fresh to eat straight away. When he talks about the herring arriving, you can sense the shadow of the shoal passing through the sea before his restaurant's windows.

Talking to cooks, chefs, fishmongers and consumers, you get a feeling that people are increasingly aware, in a positive way, of the fish food chain. Jenny Lewis at Kelynack Cornish Fish — a supplier based on the treacherous Lizard in Cornwall — sends invoices to her chefs with details of who caught the fish they are cooking. A sea bass may be 'Caught by Wilfy off The Manacles' (a notoriously dangerous group of rocks). Some of Jenny's chefs are now asking for photos of the boats that have caught the fish and also putting the names of the boats and their skippers on the menu blackboard, just as they might credit their meat producers.

The key to enjoying fish at home is, first and foremost, to go to a good fishmonger. Because fish is so perishable, and special, your efforts — and theirs — will make the difference between the wonderful and the merely OK. A proper fishmonger finds the best, and at the first whiff of age throws it out, or feeds it to the lobsters in their tanks. You only sell bad fish once, as the saying goes. You should go into such a place with an open mind and see what has swum on to the slab and looks gorgeous. It is a shame when fishmongers sell fillets off the bone on their slab. Fish is at its juiciest when cooked on the bone — and the flesh comes

'THIS BOOK NOW LANDS ITS

CATCH IN THE HARBOUR OF YOUR HANDS.'

away easily from the bones when properly cooked. Even if you want fillets, you can't admire, judge and understand the identity of a fish unless you have a sense of the whole creature. The fishmonger can then do all the preparatory work for you.

A good fishmonger is there to help shoppers and, in doing so, keep their trade: I've never met one who hasn't bent over backwards to help as much as possible, doing all the preparation you want, suggesting alternative fish for recipes, and giving simple ways to cook what is best on their slab that day. You'll know when you have found a good fishmonger: you'll want to go back.

The technique of cooking fish is simple, but requires precision. Part of the pleasure of eating seafood is the variety and succulence of its different textures, which can be lost with overcooking. Steve Harris, who runs an excellent seaside gastropub, The Sportsman, just outside Whitstable in Kent, likens fish cookery to putting on your brakes in a car. You need to start to stop before you need to stop. Get used to knowing when the fish is almost cooked, then take it off the heat – it will continue cooking for a short time until you have perfection.

The recipes in this book are organised regionally to give a sense of where fish are landed and of each fishing communities. There is nothing more special than eating fish within sight of the sea where it was caught. Of course, fishing is now an international business; we import £1.4 billion of seafood compared to the total U.K. catch, which is worth approximately £550 million. But we are an island nation that should appreciate local fish and the people who catch it.

It is to raise awareness of The Fishermen Mission's work and the lives of British fishermen that these recipes have been collected and the photographs taken. The book now lands its catch in the harbour of your hands.

SOUTH-WEST

The North Atlantic current, the Gulf Stream, the English Channel, the Irish Sea and the Bristol Channel all come together off the South-West of England, and the resulting braided mixture of temperatures, water densities and salinity helps maintain the rich biodiversity of the waters that feed many kinds of fish. Diversity is the strength of the South-West. Like a rich fish stew, the waters contain an abundance of species. Even a few tuna – known as a Mediterranean

fish – swim this way in the summer. Haddock, cod, sole, plaice, megrim, red mullet, skate, John Dory, hake, turbot, brill, whiting, gurnard, squid, scallop, octopus, cuttlefish, ling, conger eel, pollack – all could be landed from just one trawler's trip and end up on your plate. Look out, too, for the North Cornish lobsters, Cornish pilchards, line-caught mackerel, huge South Devon crabs and lemon soles auctioned in the top-notch market on the quayside at Looe.

'DIVERSITY IS THE STRENGTH OF THE SOUTH-WEST. LIKE A RICH FISH STEW THE WATERS CONTAIN AN ABUNDANCE OF SPECIES.'

SPAGHETTI WITH SEAFOOD, FRESH TOMATO, OLIVE OIL AND PARSLEY

MITCHELL TONKS, FOOD WRITER, CHEF AND 21ST CENTURY FISHMONGER, FISHWORKS, BATH, BRISTOL, CHRISTCHURCH, LONDON

'When the weather is good (and this dish is perfect for summer) fish and shellfish are plentiful,' writes Mitchell Tonks. 'Small boats can go out to sea early and make the most of the longer days, getting back for the morning's market, making the landings really fresh. This recipe is fantastic. Walk into the fishmonger's and if, like me, you can't make up your mind what to have, use a bit of everything in this dish. You can make it as cheap or as expensive as you like; the only rule is to make sure you use mussels and clams, as their juices are vital to the flavour of the sauce. I also suggest you use a firm fish such as monkfish or gurnard. If you are unsure of what to use, ask your fishmonger for advice and show him or her the recipe — he or she is there to help.'

serves 2

1 small glass dry white wine
200g mussels in their shells, scrubbed and beards removed
200g clams in their shells, scrubbed
75ml good olive oil
1 clove of garlic, peeled and chopped
6 raw prawns (get your fishmonger to peel them for you), deveined
6 raw langoustines (get your fishmonger to peel them for you), deveined
2 scallops, sliced crossways
100g monkfish fillet, sliced
6 tomatoes, skinned
small handful of parsley, chopped
sea salt and freshly ground black pepper
cooked spaghetti (let your appetite dictate, but I reckon 75g per person)

1 Put the wine in a large pan and bring to the boil. Add the mussels and clams and cover, continuing to boil. After a couple of minutes, when the shellfish have opened, remove from the heat (discard any that have not opened) and leave to cool slightly. When cool enough to handle, remove the meat from the shells and reserve the cooking liquid.

2 In a large frying pan, heat the olive oil and add the garlic, then the peeled raw prawns and langoustines, scallops and monkfish, and fry gently for 2 minutes.

3 Add the meat from the clams and mussels, then squeeze in the tomatoes, add the parsley and the cooking liquid from the clams and mussels, and simmer for 2–3 minutes. Season to taste, then add the cooked spaghetti, toss it around and serve.

ROASTED MONKFISH WITH OLIVE OIL, FENNEL, GARLIC AND ROSEMARY

MITCHELL TONKS, FOOD WRITER, CHEF AND 21ST CENTURY FISHMONGER, FISHWORKS, BATH, BRISTOL, CHRISTCHURCH, LONDON

'Although monkfish needs some help on the flavour front, its texture is fabulous,' writes Mitchell Tonks. 'The flavours in this recipe are very Mediterranean, and the fish, cooked gently in the olive oil, softens and flakes and tastes fantastic. This makes a great lunch dish served hot, or allow it to go cold and serve it as a salad. If you have a barbecue going, start the fish on it to get an outdoor smoky flavour, then put the fish in the olive oil and finish cooking it in the oven.'

serves 4

1 monkfish tail (1kg), skinned, on the bone, membrane removed
200ml good olive oil
1 tbsp fennel seeds
1 head garlic, peeled and cut in half horizontally
a few sprigs of rosemary
2–3 ripe tomatoes
small handful of basil, shredded
small handful of parsley, chopped
juice of ½ lemon
sea salt and freshly ground black pepper

1 Preheat the oven to 200°C/400°F/gas mark 6.

2 Put the monkfish in a roasting tray with the olive oil, sprinkle over the fennel seeds, then add the garlic and rosemary. Give the tomatoes a squeeze so their juices run into the oil, then add the flesh too.

3 Roast for 10–12 minutes, until you get white milky juices running from the monkfish. Remove from the oven and leave to rest for a minute or two. Stir in the basil, parsley and lemon juice, then season. Carve easily from the bone in chunks and serve with the juices.

ROASTED CORNISH MACKEREL WITH NORTH AFRICAN SPICES

MITCHELL TONKS, FOOD WRITER, CHEF AND 21ST CENTURY FISHMONGER, FISHWORKS, BATH, BRISTOL, CHRISTCHURCH, LONDON

'Mackerel is one of my favourite fish and probably one of the first that I ate,' writes Mitchell Tonks. 'It is full of flavour, but must be eaten spankingly fresh. Blues, greens and sometimes purples are the colours you should see on the back of the fish when it is at its prime. Avoid dull greys and reddened eyes — you just won't get the flavour and enjoyment. This spice mix is fabulous rubbed into the flesh and left for an hour or so to marinate. Then the fish is cooked over a hot fire so that the skin blisters and blackens. The final adornment is just a big squeeze of lemon.'

serves 2

2 mackerel, cleaned and gutted
1 tbsp cumin seeds, or ground
1 tbsp coriander seeds, or ground
1 large bunch of fresh coriander
1 large bunch of parsley
6 large cloves of garlic
1 tbsp paprika
good pinch of cayenne
juice of 2 lemons
300ml olive oil
lemon wedges, to serve
sliced red onion, to serve

1 For maximum flavour, dry-roast the whole cumin and coriander seeds yourself in a small skillet or frying pan and then grind to a fine powder.

2 Place the fresh coriander, parsley and garlic in a food processor and whiz finely. Stir in the ground cumin and coriander, paprika, cayenne and lemon juice, then beat together with the olive oil.

3 Make two or three slashes down the sides of the mackerel and rub the spice mixture in well, making sure it gets right inside the slashes. Leave for an hour or so to marinate.

4 Preheat the oven to 200°C/400°F/gas mark 6. Roast the mackerel for 8–10 minutes.

5 Serve with a good squeeze of lemon and a green salad with plenty of sliced red onion.

A TOWER OF CORNISH FISH

CLARE HOLDSWORTH, PINE COTTAGE B&B, PORTLOE, CORNWALL

This bone-free, attractive and adaptable dish is great for easy entertaining, according to the award-winning cook Clare Holdsworth. Because this dish can be made in advance, she has even prepared it for 100. Clare lives with fisherman Bill Blamey, who comes from a family that has fished from the same part of the south Cornish coast – Gerrans Bay and Veryan Bay – for 400 years. She knows her fish from sea to plate and the range of fish used in this simple recipe shows off the traditional Cornish mixed catch.

serves 4 or more

4–5 small (225–275g) pieces of fish fillet per person, eg wild salmon, brill, wild sea bass, lemon sole or red mullet, boned and skinned (reserve bones and heads, and leave the skin on the mullet)

lemon slices
olive oil
lemon juice
fresh herbs, eg thyme, fennel fronds and curly parsley
freshly ground black pepper

1 Put a slice of lemon per person in an ovenproof dish. On top of each lemon slice, layer the fish fillets, with the biggest on the bottom and the smallest on top. Start with a firm fish such as salmon or halibut. Layer up the fillets at a slight angle to each other to provide a contrast of colour and texture. After the first layer you could put a piece of brill, then some sea bass, then some lemon sole. The sole can be wrapped around your finger to make a cone. Place a piece of red mullet, skin-side-up, on top.

2 Drizzle some olive oil over the fish and squeeze over some lemon juice. Scatter over whatever fresh herbs you have to hand; Clare might use thyme, fennel fronds and parsley. Season with black pepper. You can prepare the dish up to a day in advance to this point and leave it covered in the refrigerator.

3 To make a stock, put the reserved fish bones and heads into a pan, cover with water, bring to the boil, skim and simmer for 10 minutes. Strain the stock off the bones and boil for 10 minutes or so to reduce it and concentrate the flavour. Cool and store in the refrigerator if not using immediately.

4 When you want to cook the fish, preheat the oven to 180°C/350°F/gas mark 4. About 20 minutes before serving, pour the stock over the fish and cook for 15–20 minutes in the oven.

5 Serve the fish towers by sliding a fish slice under each piece of lemon with its tower on top. The lemon, oil and stock will have emulsified to make a sauce. Pour this around the fish and, if you like, put a final flourish of parsley or another herb into each cone of sole, or on top of the red mullet.

TACTICS OF THE CATCH

Nobody lives more than 16 miles from the sea in Cornwall. Wherever you are, the breeze carries an edge of salt. For the fishermen steaming out of Newlyn, the highest-grossing fishing port in England and Wales, the land is the edge of the water as much as the other way round. There is a local phrase for passing between the massive granite arms of Newlyn harbour: you go 'through the gaps' with an empty boat, hungry for fish, and hope to come back with a holdful. This is the heart of the hunt.

What are the tactics of the catch? First find your fish. The fishermen need to know what is feeding, where and when. Humans are just the end of a long line of predators. The shoaling fish, such as mackerel, go after the smaller fish that feed on the plankton. The shoals will in turn attract the fish that feed on them, the predatory species such as tuna, hake and whiting. The detritus from this fish feast falls to the seabed, where it fattens up shellfish, such as crabs and lobsters. They, in turn, can be eaten by fish when they shed their shells and become soft and vulnerable. And so it goes on, though climate, biology and humans affect the links in this aquatic food chain.

The fishermen must know the contours of seabed, with its rocky, sandy, rough and smooth floor in forms as different as fields, valleys and hills. Wrecks and rocky grounds can prove fecund. Fish gather and come close to the shore when they are spawning, and these breeding patterns are important to fishermen, and not just because it makes the fish easier to catch in quantity. Most fish are at their peak before releasing their eggs and afterwards become thin and watery, or 'slinky', fetching a lower price.

Before technology surpassed intuition and knowledge, fishermen had to read the sea like a book. Those fishing within a couple of miles of the shore lined up landmarks to pinpoint a favourite spot, and their phrases formed an oral geography handed down through generations. They noticed birds also after fish. Particular weather conditions made for good or bad fishing: 'When the wind's in the east, the fish bite the least.' You could forecast weather by small changes in the sea, and such skills saved many a life.

Using Global Positioning Systems, fishermen can get to the exact spot they want and sonar helps track their quarry. For all such tools, to the seaman the water is still infinitely varied and patterned. A good fisherman remembers what was good, where and in what circumstances, and goes back to the right place at the right time. Some skippers do better than others through a combination of knowledge, skill and determination. And some boats try to follow the successful to their hot spots. There is an element of human hide-and-seek even in this most open of spaces.

Different fish can be targeted with different fishing gear. Fixed equipment involves putting out lines, pots or nets, leaving them in the sea, and collecting what is caught when the fish take the bait on the lines. Shellfish are lured into the pots, or fish swim into the nets and are tangled up or caught by their gills. Towed or trawled gear catches fish in a big net, funnelling them down to the 'cod' end, while seine nets encircle shoals. Nets can be adjusted to catch fish swimming at the bottom of the sea, such as flat fish, and those that swim mid water, such as mackerel.

Smaller boats may use a variety of methods over the year, including netting for spider crabs and shooting pots for lobsters. There are men who use handlines for mackerel and sea bass, both of which are now marketed as line-caught fish and get a premium because they're in peak condition. Some fishmongers label fish from 'day boats', vessels that go out in the morning and return at night with very fresh fish.

Whether a trip is long or short, timing is crucial. Spring tides (strong, big tides) can tangle up gear, such as gill nets, making it unworkable. Rough weather is dangerous, but can bring greater rewards. When few go out, your catch should cash in well at the market. On more favourable days, a big haul may bring a disappointing return if others have caught the same quantity, glutting the market so the price goes down.

Everything in fishing involves risk. It is the antithesis of the landlubbers' world of salaries and health-and-safety regs. One of the biggest areas of uncertainty is how little we know about the fish and the sea. For all the tactics and technology, this natural world is still unfathomable.

TOP, LEFT TO RIGHT **Part of the Newlyn under 10-metre fleet; shellfish pots in Newlyn harbour; mending shellfish nets;** BELOW **Buoys for supporting nets aboard the netter Blejan Eyhre, owned by skipper Martin Jones, in Newlyn harbour.**

A huer's hut, from which people spotted the cloud of a shoal in the sea and signalled to the fishermen where to row their boats.

CORNISH MARIOS

NICK HOWELL, THE PILCHARD WORKS, NEWLYN, CORNWALL

Pilchards, or adult sardines, were once such a mainstay of the Cornish economy that some of Cornwall's picturesque harbours were founded on them. Then their numbers fell off and people stopped eating and catching these oily beauties. When Nick Howell started their revival in 1997, the one local boat landing pilchards was selling them for just 1½p per kilogram on the market. Nick rebranded the fish as the healthy and delicious 'Cornish sardine', and sells them fresh and carefully canned. There are now 18 local boats getting up to £1.20 per kilo for pilchards caught in a small, sustainable fishery. Many people like to grill fresh pilchards but, because they are caught in huge shoals, the Cornish have also developed preservation recipes, including this one from 1753, found in a 1928 W.I. cookbook.

serves 12

24 pilchards, scaled, headed and gutted

24 bay leaves
white wine vinegar
1 tbsp soft brown sugar
¼ tsp ground allspice

1 Preheat the oven to 150°C/300°F/gas mark 2. Put a bay leaf in the centre of each pilchard and put all the fish in a shallow ovenproof dish.

2 Cover the fish with a 50/50 mixture of water and vinegar: the quantities will depend on the size of your dish.

3 Sprinkle the sugar and allspice into the liquid. Cover the dish with brown paper, foil or a lid, and put into the preheated oven for 10 minutes, then lower the oven temperature to 110°C/225°F/gas mark ¼ and cook for a further 7 hours. By this time most of the bones will have melted away and the fillets will fall off the backbones.

4 Cornish marios can be kept in the liquid, covered, in the refrigerator for 3 weeks and are delicious with just good bread or in a salad.

BRILL WITH SORREL SAUCE AND CRISPY SPINACH

ARTHUR WATSON, RESTAURATEUR, THE RIVERSIDE, WEST BAY, DORSET

'Brill was once a neglected fish in the UK and was known as "poorman's turbot",' writes Arthur Watson, the owner of the long-standing seafood restaurant, The Riverside. 'Now it is highly prized and commands an equal price. It is very delicate and careful cooking is well rewarded. Sorrel sauce is an ideal accompaniment, as long as it is not too intense. We originally gathered our sea spinach from the upper slopes of the Chesil Beach and from local clifftops, but it is now protected and we have found an adequate substitute in the spinach grown at Sea Spray Farm, West Bexington, by Michael Michaud. It has a distinct tang of the sea.'

serves 4

fillets of brill (at least 170g per
    person), skin on
olive oil, for frying

for the sorrel sauce
300ml fish stock
4 shallots, peeled and finely diced
130ml dry white wine

juice of ½ lemon
300ml double cream
100g fresh sorrel leaves
freshly ground black pepper

for the crispy spinach
225g fresh leaf spinach
vegetable oil, for frying
salt and caster sugar, to taste

1 To make the sauce, put the fish stock, shallot, white wine and lemon juice in a heavy-bottomed pan. Bring to the boil and reduce over a high heat until the shallot is just holding the liquid.

2 Add the cream and reduce until the sauce has thickened slightly. Remove the pan from the heat, add the sorrel and blitz with a hand-held blender or in a liquidizer.

3 To make the crispy spinach, roll the spinach tightly and shred finely. Heat the oil in a large pan to 180°C/350°F and deep-fry the spinach in four batches for about 3–4 minutes each, until crisp. Stand clear; it can spit. Spread out on kitchen paper on a tray and lightly sprinkle with salt and caster sugar to taste.

4 Cook the fish in a frying pan in a little olive oil, frying each fillet skin-side down for 4–5 minutes, then on the other side for 3–4 minutes. Season with salt and pepper, and serve with the crispy spinach and the reheated sorrel sauce.

DEVILLED CRAB-STUFFED MUSHROOMS

PHILIP RIDGE, CHEF, THE OYSTER SHACK, NEAR BIGBURY-ON-SEA, DEVON

The Oyster Shack is a delightfully informal BYO seafood restaurant near Bigbury-on-Sea in the South Hams of Devon. The crabs caught in this area are famous for their size — a large cock crab can have a body the size of a piece of A4 paper. They taste great and are caught by a carefully monitored inshore fishery. The quantities given for the ingredients in this recipe are an approximation: vary them according to your taste. Always use hand-picked crab meat, says Philip Ridge, The Oyster Shack's chef.

serves 4 as a starter

knob of unsalted butter, plus extra for frying
1 shallot, peeled and finely diced
dash of Worcestershire sauce
pinch of cayenne
1 large strip unwaxed lemon zest, finely chopped
4 tbsp fresh crab meat (3 brown, 1 white)
1 tbsp grated Cheddar cheese
1 tbsp double cream
2 tbsp parsley, finely chopped
big squirt of lemon juice
dash of brandy
pinch of mustard powder
home-made breadcrumbs, to bind if necessary, plus extra for coating
12 mushrooms, about 5cm in diameter, stalks removed
plain flour
1 beaten free-range egg
olive oil, for frying
salad leaves, to serve
lemon wedges, to serve

1 Melt the butter in a pan and then gently sweat the shallot until soft, but not coloured.

2 Add the Worcestershire sauce, cayenne and lemon zest. Stir in the crab meat, breaking up any large lumps, then the cheese, cream, parsley, lemon juice, brandy and mustard powder. Check the seasoning. Stir continuously until just simmering, remove from the heat and, if necessary, add sufficient breadcrumbs for the mix, to be bound together (it depends upon the consistency of the crab meat), and leave to cool.

3 Stuff each mushroom with the crab mixture so it is just concave (about 1 tsp of mixture per mushroom). Dip each stuffed mushroom in turn into the flour, then the egg, then the breadcrumbs.

4 Part shallow-fry and part grill (or turn over gently in the pan) in a mixture olive oil and a little butter until lightly brown and crispy on both sides.

5 Serve three mushrooms per person on some salad leaves dressed with a little olive oil and lemon juice, and a lemon wedge. Pour the hot oil from the pan over the mushrooms and serve with a large glass of Sauvignon Blanc.

CITRUS JOHN DORY

DAN THE FISH MAN, FISH SELLER AND PROMOTER, DEVON

Clovelly-based Dan Garnett believes there is a future for fish in small-scale, local markets where you get genuine contact and trust between customer and fish merchant. His mobile fish stall consists of an 'Edwardian' fish barrow, pulled by a van which he takes around the markets of North Devon in Hatherleigh, Holsworthy, South Molton and Bideford. Although he will get fish from further afield, he concentrates almost entirely on what is caught by 17 small local boats, including the special Clovelly herring that are caught in Bideford Bay between late autumn and Christmas Eve. Most of Dan's fish are sold no more than an hour's drive from where they were landed. He also visits schools, runs workshops with community groups and has set up an occasional Saturday lunch club for local fish lovers.

serves 4

4 medium John Dory (about 450g each), gutted and trimmed (ask your fishmonger to side-trim the fish, taking off the spikes and trimming the frilly bits)

a little olive oil
juice of ½ lemon
2 small glasses white wine
sea salt and freshly ground black pepper
2 large tbsp crème fraîche
segments of 1 pink grapefruit, warmed, to serve

1 Preheat the oven to 220°C/425°F/gas mark 7.

2 Dribble a little olive oil on an ovenproof dish. Put the John Dory on top. Pour over the lemon juice and a glass of the white wine, and season with sea salt and black pepper.

3 Put the fish in the hot oven for 5 minutes, then cover with foil and give them 10 more minutes. To test if the fish is cooked, put a skewer or knife into the thickest part of it and, if the flesh is still a touch bloody by the backbone, put the fish back in the oven for another 5 minutes.

4 Pour the juices from the dish into a saucepan, add the other glass of wine and boil over a high heat to reduce by half. Take off the heat and stir in the crème fraîche.

5 Serve the fish with the sauce accompanied with warmed pink grapefruit segments, steamed new potatoes and a selection of seasonal vegetables. This dish can also be made with large red gurnard fillets, and you can substitute the pink grapefruit with halved seedless black or white grapes, adding them to the sauce at the last minute.

VICHYSSOISE WITH OYSTER CROUTONS

HUGH FEARNLEY-WHITTINGSTALL, FOOD WRITER AND BROADCASTER

Native oysters are good when there is an 'r' in the month. During the summer they are spawning and out of season. Pacific, or rock, oysters, however, can be eaten all year round, and you can use either for this elegant dish.

serves 6

50g unsalted butter
3–4 leeks (white only), sliced
500g floury potatoes, peeled and cut into large chunks
1 litre chicken, fish or vegetable stock
pinch of curry powder
2 tbsp double cream
sea salt and freshly ground black pepper

for the croûtons

6 thin slices white or brown bread
olive oil or clarified butter
large wine glass white wine
large wine glass water
knob of unsalted butter
2 oysters per person
1 tbsp double cream
a couple of handfuls of chives or chervil, finely chopped

1 Melt the butter in a large pan and sweat the leeks in it until soft. Add the potato and stock. Bring to the boil and simmer until the potato is cooked. Remove the potato and rub through a sieve.

2 Purée the leek and potato in a blender with a little stock and the curry powder until smooth. Put everything back in the pan and stir in 2 tbsp double cream. Season with salt and pepper to taste.

3 Stamp out small rounds of bread and fry them gently in olive oil or clarified butter until brown. Keep warm until ready to use.

4 Put the wine, water and butter in a large pan and bring to the boil. Put the closed oysters in the pan, cover with a lid and cook for 2 minutes. Remove the whole oysters carefully from the shells and pour the juices back into the pan.

5 Make a garnishing sauce with the wine and oyster-poaching juices by straining them through muslin or a new j-cloth and boiling to reduce to about 2–3 tbsp. Add 1 tbsp double cream and boil until thick and glossy. Remove from the heat and add a handful of finely chopped herbs.

6 To serve, reheat the soup, without boiling, and ladle it into bowls. Put an oyster on each bread croûton and place these on top of the soup. Spoon over a little sauce and garnish with more chopped chives or chervil.

SCANDINAVIAN-CURED MACKEREL

HUGH FEARNLEY-WHITTINGSTALL, FOOD WRITER AND BROADCASTER

Mackerel are often cheap and plentiful — in the summer, fishermen and fishmongers practically give them away — and this is an ideal way to mop up a glut, using the same process of curing fish that is employed for salmon in gravadlax.

serves 10

10 very fresh mackerel, filleted, skin on

for the cure
100g caster sugar
75g coarse salt
15g coarsely ground black or white pepper
1 large bunch of dill (the best you can find), large stalks removed, finely chopped

for the curing box
Hugh uses an old half-bottle wooden wine crate, which is naturally leaky: the juice seeps out between the pieces of wood. You could also use a big plastic box, with a few holes pierced through the bottom of both ends. Another handy option – one without holes – is to use the salad drawer in the bottom of the refrigerator, with one end wedged up slightly with some newspaper. The idea behind all these methods is that the fish should not stew in its own juices. Then you need a plastic or wooden chopping board that fits inside. Do not use a metal container or board and if you use a metal weight do not let it touch the cure or fish because it will spoil the flavour.

for the sauce
4 tsp English mustard
2 tsp white wine vinegar
4 tsp caster or light brown sugar
6 tbsp crème fraîche
2–4 tbsp chopped fresh dill

1 In a non-metallic bowl, mix together all the cure ingredients. Sprinkle just a little of the mixture over the base of your curing box. Place a layer of mackerel fillets on top, skin-side down, with the thin edges just overlapping. Spoon over a little more of the cure and place the next layer on top, skin-side up. Repeat until you have used all your fillets.

2 Put a board over the fish and weigh it down with heavy weights, such as a couple of bricks or some heavy jars. If using a curing box with holes, put it on a non-metallic tray to catch any leaking liquid. Leave in a cool place, such as a refrigerator or larder, and baste once a day by removing the board and spooning over the liquid that has leaked out, or if you are using the salad drawer or a box without holes, just pour the liquid out and spoon it back over.

3 The 'gravadmax' can be eaten in two or three days. Cut each fillet into three or four thin slices with a sharp knife, cutting on an angle to remove the flesh from the skin.

4 To make the sauce, mix the mustard, vinegar and sugar, then add the crème fraîche and dill. Serve the fish with the sauce, salad, bread and butter.

POLLACK IN BEER BATTER

HUGH FEARNLEY-WHITTINGSTALL, FOOD WRITER AND BROADCASTER

Pollack is an underrated fish that is coming into its own as people look for alternatives to cod. As with cod, and other fish such as ling, whiting and coley, its texture benefits from an initial sprinkling of salt, as in this recipe for a British classic. 'I don't always want chips with my battered fish, but I do like mushy peas and tartare sauce,' writes Hugh.

serves 4

4 pollack fillets (up to 255g each), or any other good white fish
200g plain flour
salt and freshly ground black pepper
2 tbsp olive or groundnut oil
255ml beer
2 tbsp extra flaky or coarse sea salt
groundnut oil, for deep-frying
2 free-range egg whites

1 Sift the flour into a bowl and season with a little salt and pepper. Mix in 2 tbsp oil and then stir in 225ml beer a little at a time. Leave to rest whilst you prepare the fish.

2 Put a layer of flaky or coarse sea salt on a chopping board. Put the fish skin-side down on the salt (you can use skinned fillets if you prefer). Sprinkle another layer of salt on top. Leave for 15 minutes. Rinse off the salt under cold running water and pat dry with kitchen paper. Season with a little black pepper and leave for 10 minutes.

3 Heat the groundnut oil, around 10cm deep, in a pan to 160°C/310°F.

4 Whisk the egg whites until they form stiff peaks. Loosen the batter with 2 tbsp beer and fold in the whisked whites. Dip a fillet of fish into the batter, then lower carefully into the hot oil. Deep-fry for about 4–5 minutes, turning over once, until the batter is golden brown. Carefully remove with a large deep-frying basket. Put on a warmed dish lined with a few layers of kitchen paper and leave in a warm place. Cook each fillet like this in turn.

CORNISH BLUE LOBSTER SALAD NICOISE WITH SEARED TUNA

GRANT NETHERCOTT, CHEF-PATRON, ALBA, ST IVES, CORNWALL

Alba, an AA seafood restaurant of the year, sits on the harbour at St Ives. After 12 years cooking in the area, Grant Nethercott has forged links with a wide network of local producers. Most of his fish comes from the excellent local fish merchant Matthew Stevens, and he also buys lobsters straight from the boat of a local fisherman, Glynn Farrell. He tries to find ways of making lobster more accessible on a reasonably priced menu, and this is one result. He thinks buying smaller lobsters means getting sweeter meat.

serves 4

450–680g lobster
450g tuna loin, trimmed by your fishmonger into a cylindrical shape
olive oil
Maldon sea salt and freshly ground black pepper

for the poaching liquid
1 carrot, finely diced
1 onion, peeled and finely diced
1 stick of celery, finely diced
1 bay leaf
a few parsley sprigs
6 black peppercorns
1 tbsp salt
water

for the salad Niçoise
24 fine green beans, cooked in boiling water for 2 minutes
8 salted anchovy fillets, cut into a fine julienne
6 quail eggs, boiled for 1 minute, peeled and halved
6 vine baby plum tomatoes, halved
12 Niçoise black olives (or similar), stoned
30g baby capers
12 small new potatoes, cooked and halved
30g baby wild rocket

for the vinaigrette
3 tbsp sherry vinegar
1 tsp Dijon mustard
3 tbsp extra-virgin olive oil, plus extra for drizzling

1. Put all the poaching liquid ingredients into a pan with enough water to cover the lobster. Bring to the boil and add the lobster. Bring back to the boil and cook for 6 minutes. Allow the lobster to cool in the liquid.

2. When the lobster is cool, remove the tail meat from the shell and the meat from the claws, cracking them open using a nutcracker or the back of a large, heavy knife. Remove the intestine from the tail meat. Chop the meat into pieces roughly the same size as the halved baby tomatoes. Cool and keep chilled in the refrigerator.

3. Fry the tuna on each side for 30 seconds in a hot pan in a little olive oil. Cool. Roll tightly in cling film and chill for at least a couple of hours.

4. In a large bowl, combine all Niçoise salad ingredients and the lobster meat.

5. Whisk together the vinaigrette ingredients and dress the salad, then season with salt and pepper. Arrange on plates.

6. Slice the tuna as thinly as you can to get three or four slices per person. Arrange on the top of the salad. Drizzle with extra-virgin olive oil and season with twist of black pepper and a sprinkle of Maldon sea salt.

TOPE WITH A WILD MUSHROOM AND TARRAGON SAUCE

TINA BRICKNELL-WEBB, CHEF-PATRON, PERCY'S, VIRGINSTOW, DEVON

'Tope is a member of the shark family,' writes Tina Bricknell-Webb. 'It is a fish I first encountered in 1989, when a large consignment was landed and shipped to Billingsgate; we now buy it at Looe fish market. I had absolutely no idea how to cook this fish, so I braised, baked, grilled, fried and steamed various fillets until I plumped for the pan-fried option. In those days I had a kitchen manned by a handful of Sri Lankans who had well-developed palates, and one of them said tope tasted very much like chicken. It does have a firm, meaty texture that can take strong flavours. I had just taken delivery of a selection of very fresh wild mushrooms and had some chicken stock simmering. This dish is the result of one of my trials and lots of tasters.'

serves 4

4 x 170g tope steaks, skinned
2.8 litres chicken stock
1 heaped tbsp cornflour
sea salt and freshly ground black pepper
450g mixed wild mushrooms (oyster, wood hedgehog, blewitts and ceps), stalks removed
olive oil, for frying
cornmeal, for dusting the fish
60ml clarified butter or olive or avocado oil, for frying
250g crème fraîche
juice of 1 lemon
1–2 tbsp chopped fresh tarragon, to taste

1. Reduce the chicken stock by boiling it until you have 550ml left. Stir the cornflour into a little cold water, then add to the stock to thicken it, stirring. Place the tope steaks on a board. Sprinkle both sides with a little sea salt. Leave to rest for 10 minutes.

2. Meanwhile, pick over the mushroom tops (do not use the stalks). Tear them, with the grain, into bite-size pieces. Heat a little olive oil in a wok or non-stick pan, then toss the mushrooms in the oil until soft.

3. Rinse the salt off the steaks, pat them dry, then dredge them in the cornmeal. Heat a heavy skillet and pour in the clarified butter or oil. When hot but not smoking, add the tope and fry until lightly coloured on both sides. Turn down the heat and cook very gently until the steaks are cooked through. To tell when the fish is ready, press gently down on it, taking care not to break the cornmeal crust, and you should just feel the flakes give a little. The fish will continue to cook a little when you take it off the heat.

4. As the fish is cooking, bring the reduced stock to the boil. Add the crème fraîche, lemon juice, black pepper to taste and mushrooms. Simmer until it has reduced slightly and add the tarragon just before serving. You'll need less of home-grown, fresh pungent tarragon than you will of shop-bought.

5. Serve with mashed potato cooked with tarragon stalks in the water, or steamed rice mixed with a little avocado oil, black pepper and chopped tarragon and a large tossed salad with an avocado oil vinaigrette.

LOOE LEMON SOLE WITH CORNISH CIDER

IAN MURRAY, FISHERMAN AND CHEF, BARCLAY HOUSE, LOOE, CORNWALL

Ian Murray fished for 28 years and still lives in Cawsand, a fishing village near Plymouth, where he first served his apprenticeship on a cousin's boat (suffering seasickness every day for the first couple of months: some fishermen never entirely get over this affliction). Ian now works as head chef at Barclay House, near the fish market at Looe, which is famous for its landings of magnificent lemon sole, at their very best from January to May. 'Never drown a fish in a sauce' is one of Ian's cooking mottos: he likes to present the two side by side on the plate. In this recipe, he uses the Cornish Orchard Cider from Duloe up the road, Cornish cream and fish from the nearby harbour.

serves 4

4 fillets of lemon sole (175–225g per person), skin on
1 shallot, peeled and finely chopped
1 tsp olive oil, plus extra for brushing
1–2 tsp Madras curry powder
2 wine glasses of cider
300ml Cornish double cream
sea salt and ground white pepper
mashed potato, to serve

1. Fry the shallot in the olive oil for a couple of minutes over a medium heat, until starting to brown.

2. Sprinkle the shallot with the curry powder.

3. Pour the cider into the pan, stirring so you scrape up the residue on the bottom of the pan. Bring to the boil and reduce by half.

4. Add the cream, bring briefly to the boil, and season with salt and white pepper. If needed, add more cider for sweetness, and extra curry powder if the dish requires more fragrance. You can make the sauce a little in advance and keep it hot in a bain-marie until you are ready to cook the fish if you wish.

5. Lightly season the fish with salt and white pepper. Brush the fillets with a little olive oil and put them under a hot grill, or on a hot griddle, flesh-side down, for 2–3 minutes. This is the presentation side and you want it to brown slightly. Turn the fillets over and cook for another 30–60 seconds to get a little bit of colour. Take the fish off the heat; the fillets will continue to cook slightly.

6. To serve, put the fish skin-side down on a spoonful of mash and surround with the sauce. Serve with vegetables such as baton carrots and fine green beans or sugar snap peas.

SOUTH-EAST

On the south coast, so close and so far from metropolitan life, fishermen continue their business, bringing the rhythm of the sea into towns and cities as their catch varies with time and tide. You can learn through the fishmongers what is best to buy when, and enjoy treats such as the Rye Bay scallops and the plump autumn plaice that feed up on the mussel banks in the English Channel during the season. Days out by the seaside, in the balmy

summer or bracing winter, can bring pint-pots of shellfish, barbecued mackerel or a New Year's Day 'hangover-cure' fish soup, in places such as Hastings' Old Town and Brighton's fishing quarter. At Hastings, the fishing boats are still winched on and off the shingle beach. Although gear is no longer hung in the tall net sheds that stand on the Old Town beach, The Stade, the structures stand guard on tradition like sentry boxes, and a fishing museum connects the past to the present.

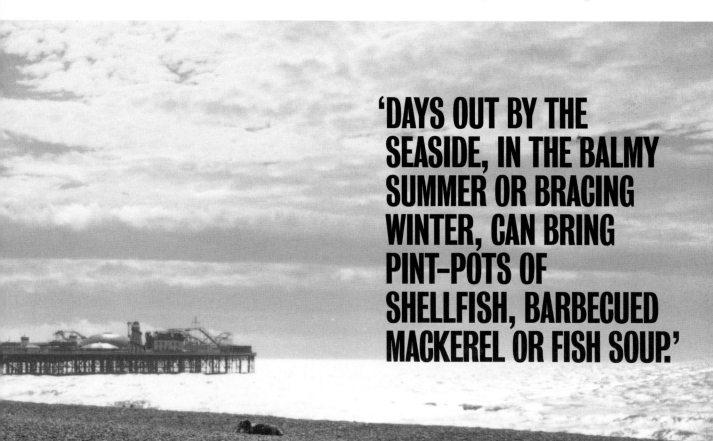

'DAYS OUT BY THE SEASIDE, IN THE BALMY SUMMER OR BRACING WINTER, CAN BRING PINT-POTS OF SHELLFISH, BARBECUED MACKEREL OR FISH SOUP.'

TURBOT FILLET BRAISED IN VIN JAUNE AND MORELS

STEVE HARRIS, CHEF-PATRON, THE SPORTSMAN, SEASALTER, NEAR WHITSTABLE, KENT

'As anyone who cooks with turbot knows, it has a texture more akin to meat than fish,' writes Steve Harris of The Sportsman gastropub on the Kent coast at Seasalter, near Whitstable. 'This dish was inspired by the chicken leg with vin jaune and morels, that was on early Nico Ladenis menus. At the same time, I was noticing how Marco Pierre White's fish dishes were very quick and last minute, and came up with a blend of the two ideas. The result is a very curious sauce that seems to send people into a spin. I put this down to the fact that it is a flavour combination that most people have never had before and so their brains are working overtime to try to analyse the taste. I have been asked if I add cheese or coffee to it! Vin jaune is a slightly oxidized sherry-style French wine. You could substitute it with Noilly Prat or fino sherry.'

serves 4

20 dried morels
unsalted butter, softened
sea salt
4 x 175g turbot fillets, skinned
about 3 tbsp vin jaune (or Noilly Prat or fino sherry)
1 small ladle (about 50ml) of fish velouté
juice of ½ lemon

1 Prepare the dried morels by putting them in a sieve and washing them under the hot-water tap to remove the grit. Leave them damp but covered for at least half an hour. Do not reconstitute them more than this. They will later be soaking in the vin jaune and if you leave them in water at this stage they can become spongy and tasteless.

2 Spread a thin layer of unsalted butter in a non-stick baking tray that is big enough to hold the fillets so they fit quite snugly, and sprinkle with a pinch of sea salt. Put the turbot fillets on top and pour over a healthy glug of vin jaune. Add the morels. Leave the vin jaune, turbot and morels to sit, covered, for 15 minutes.

3 Preheat the oven to 170°C/325°F/gas mark 3.

4 Sprinkle a little more sea salt on the fish and put a knob of butter on top, then cook the fish, morels and vin jaune gently in the oven for 10 minutes, or until just cooked. To check this, pick up a fillet with a fish slice and bend it open gently to see if it is almost cooked through. A millimetre or two of rawness in the middle will continue cooking in the residual heat as you make the sauce. Transfer the morels to a pan.

5 Put the fish velouté in the pan with the morels and boil rapidly. Add another 30g butter and cook, stirring, until the sauce develops a consistency that coats the back of a spoon. Check the seasoning and add the lemon juice.

6 To serve, put the fish on some greens or cabbage, and pour the sauce over the fish. Serve with some potatoes, such as mash or boiled pink fir apple potatoes.

SCALLOPS WITH AN ORANGE AND VERMOUTH SAUCE

TONI FERGUSON-LEES, CHEF-PATRON, RYE'S LANDGATE BISTRO, RYE BAY, EAST SUSSEX

When Rye Bay's plump scallops are in season from November to Easter, Toni Ferguson-Lees, chef–owner of Rye's Landgate Bistro, uses them in this simple, classic dish. She always buys them live, in the shell. When the scallops are this fresh, they have a sweetness that is brought out by this sauce. If scallop prices are high, she says, you could economize by replacing half of them with fillets from a firm white fish such as brill.

serves 4 as a main course

3–4 scallops per person
olive oil
zest and juice of 1 unwaxed
    orange
large wine glass of vermouth
    (Noilly Prat)
large wine glass of fish stock
knob (about 30g) of salted
    butter
freshly ground black pepper

1 If you are using scallops in the shell, prepare them in the following way. Hold the shell flat-side up in the palm of one hand. Slide a knife into the shell and run it along the flat side of the shell about half-way down, to cut through the ligament attaching the meat to the shell. Once this is severed, the scallop opens up. Cut the ligament away completely. Pull off the scallop's skirt and the rest of the gubbins so you are left with the scallop and roe. Wash. Cut the roe free and discard the little bit of sinew between it and the white meat.

2 Cut each scallop in half, horizontally, to get two flat discs.

3 Heat a griddle or a heavy frying pan on a high flame for 5 minutes. Brush with oil.

4 Quickly cook the scallops and roes on the griddle, turning them over once. Each should take less than a minute. Cook them in two or three batches, if necessary, rather than overcrowding the griddle and bringing its temperature down. Put the scallops in a warm place while you quickly make the sauce.

5 Pour the orange zest and juice, vermouth and fish stock into the pan, letting the alcohol burn off and the sauce reduce down and thicken. The sauce will have a lovely caramelized flavour. Thicken with a knob of butter and season with freshly ground black pepper.

6 Serve the scallops with the sauce and either seasonal vegetables or a salad, and new potatoes, or mashed potatoes if you feel like comfort food.

SLOW-COOKED SQUID

TED GILLAM, FISHERMAN, BRIGHTON, SUSSEX

Brighton fisherman Ted Gillam has a family name that goes back to the Domesday Book, and it is possible Gillams have been fishing from this time. Ted is an inshore fisherman and goes out, weather permitting, at around 5a.m. every day and fishes usually around three to four miles off the coast, although he may go out as far as 12 miles. One day he puts out trammel nets, which are fixed to the seabed, then he collects what has been caught the next day and puts out more nets. Dover sole, plaice and cod provide most of his income, but he is delighted when squid accidentally get caught in his nets and he can take them home to simmer to tenderness in a slow cooker.

serves 4

1kg squid
vegetable oil, for stir-frying
1 large onion, peeled and roughly chopped
2 cloves of garlic, peeled and crushed or chopped
1 tsp or more chilli powder, to taste
handful of basil, shredded
400g tinned chopped tomatoes
150ml red wine
150ml water

1 To prepare the squid, take everything out of the body, chop off the tentacles just below the head, and discard the rest, including the beak above the tentacles, the ink sac and the quill. Give the body a good wash and peel off the thin membrane.

2 Cut the body into 1cm rings and the tentacles into 1cm lengths.

3 Heat a little oil in a wok and stir-fry the squid until slightly patched with brown. Add the onion and garlic, and stir-fry for 5 minutes to soften. Add the chilli powder, basil, tomatoes, wine and water.

4 Preheat the oven to 150°C/300°F/gas mark 2. Put the mixture into an ovenproof dish and cook in the low oven for 1½–2 hours until tender. Serve with rice or potatoes and a green salad.

TOP, LEFT TO RIGHT **Freia and Nigel Sayers** in front of their original Brighton shop; fishing boats in Brighton marina.
FAR RIGHT AND BELOW Brighton's fishing quarter, with fish sellers, a fishing museum, a smokehouse and historic boats.

TWO FISHMONGERS

Nigel and Freia Sayers advertise their trade with a one-and-a-half metre papier mâché mackerel in the front of their Brighton shop, N. Sayers Fish Merchants. The stainless-steel counter gleams with fish amid crisp ice. The iridescent red mullet, the chain mail of black bream, the famous Dover sole, brill, tender squid, lemon sole, sea bass and more are all landed locally. Nigel worked as a fisherman for 10 years, first on trawlers fishing out of Newhaven, then on inshore boats. Then he became a 'boy ashore', as the Sussex saying goes, and set up this modern fishmongers with his wife Freia, first in Kemptown and now in the fishing quarter of Brighton's seafront, in arches where they used to keep nets for their boat. Together they have made a contemporary shop with an emphasis on ingredients.

Freia grew up in Hong Kong and they have both travelled extensively, absorbing the Asian love of freshness and spices. People feel happy to ask questions in this friendly shop, and she and Nigel give advice on ways to cook the fish, whether as easy fast food, flashed in and out of the pan or oven, with olive oil, sea salt and lemon juice, or something smart and simple such as a steamed black bream stuffed with ginger, spring onions and a touch of garlic.

Alongside loving the quality of the fish, Brighton's switched-on customers come here because of the Sayers' environmental stance. The couple sell what is seasonal and local as much as possible. They won't sell scallops in summer, when they are spawning, preferring, like the French, to have a closed season. They won't sell cod, monkfish, skate, swordfish or bluefin tuna. The salmon is wild or organic.

The customers, says Freia, are increasingly educated and excited about fish. Young people come in eager to know more and ready to ask questions. Fewer people come in with a fixed idea of what they want. More and more want to see what is best on the day and cook accordingly.

Half an hour's drive away, in a shopping precinct in the village of Ringmer on the outskirts of Lewes, George Lillicrap sets out his fish stall on Tuesday and Friday mornings. He modestly calls his operation a 'jing-bang' outfit because of its scale, yet it's as trim and proud as a small sea trout.

George, aged 72, is a salt-of-the-sea, with blue eyes that have seen horizons. In the summer the fish, picked up daily from Hastings, will be iced in polystyrene boxes in the back of his open pick-up truck, with a piece of ticking stretched over, and a striped umbrella for shade. A fold-up table stands ready to one side, with a chopping board and two knives, a nailbrush, a bucket of water, a bucket for offcuts, and a Thermos of hot water. There may also be bags of cherry buns. The fish and bunches of herbs and Swiss chard from George's garden are wrapped in newspaper donated by neighbours and customers. A piece of haddock, perhaps from the tasty tail end, might be wrapped in the FT, or the International Herald Tribune.

One of the most important things to consider when buying fish, apart from freshness, George says, is its season. Customers can get a better deal if they know when a fish is at its peak. You also get the enjoyment of returning seasons. His personal favourites are scallops in January and herring that can arrive up until Christmas – '... if we're lucky, depending on weather and the fish, and the fact that they don't like to land them because the English don't eat them and the price is low, which is a crying shame' – and Dover sole. The Dovers, the mainstay of the Channel fishery, are pretty good all year round. Plaice, in contrast, spawn over Christmas, and there isn't much for them to eat so they only really recover their weight again in March.

George gets up at 3.45a.m. every morning to go to Hastings to buy his fish, and has done for 38 years. He watches the winds on this part of the south coast: when they are from the east or south-east, the Hastings shore boats cannot land and some of the fish he buys on the market must come from further afield. He used to have a boat himself, in Newhaven, and he still smokes fish at home. As another sideline, George has taught the opera chorus at nearby Glyndebourne how to gut herring and mend nets on stage for Benjamin Britten's 'Peter Grimes'.

These two fish-sellers epitomize the quality and character of the independent retailer; it is crucial to consumers that this breed survives.

'DAB-IN-A-BUN' (OR FISHERMAN'S ROLL)

TUSH AND PAT HAMILTON, FISH SELLERS AND PROMOTERS, HASTINGS, SUSSEX

The Hamiltons have been in the seafood game most of their lives and promote the variety and quality of British fish. During the summer holidays and on fine weekends between February and October they can be found near the fishing museum in Rock-a-Nore Road in the Old Town of Hastings, frying up whatever has just been caught locally. They offer customers two or three pieces of different fish, fried in olive oil in a big paella pan and served in a roll. Tush's favourite fish for the contents is dab, a small flat fish that's underrated, plentiful, and therefore a bargain.

per person

2–3 fillets of fish (perhaps a piece of gurnard, plaice and dab), skinned

olive oil
plain flour
1 white roll
lemon juice or vinegar, optional

1 Heat a little olive oil in a frying pan. Toss the fish fillets in some flour.

2 Fry the fish for 2–3 minutes, skin-side down. Turn the fillets over and give them another minute on the other side. The exact timing will depend on the size of fillets.

3 Put in the bun with a squeeze of lemon or a few drops of vinegar, if desired.

SOUTH COAST FISH SOUP

RICKY HODGSON, CHEF, DUE SOUTH, BRIGHTON, SUSSEX

Ricky Hodgson is the chef at Due South, a restaurant housed in former fishing-net arches on Brighton seafront. His cooking is based on local, seasonal produce, including daily deliveries of fish landed just along the coast at Shoreham. He writes: 'The amounts and types of fish used in this recipe are open to interpretation with regards to what individuals choose to put in; it will always taste lovely!'

serves 6 as a starter, 4 as a
  main course

about 1kg fish fillets from
  4 different kinds of fish,
  skinned and boned
1 medium onion, peeled and
  finely diced
1 carrot, finely diced
1 stick celery, finely diced
½ bulb of fennel, finely diced
a little olive oil
2 cloves of garlic, peeled and
  crushed
40g tomato purée
¼ bottle white wine (about
  200ml)
pinch of saffron
1 bay leaf
750ml good fish stock
30 mussels in their shells,
  scrubbed and beards removed

18 cockles
knob of butter
chopped flat-leaf parsley, to
  garnish

Some of the fish you could use
  that are generally available
  on the South coast: mussels
  (from Poole); cockles;
  mackerel (late spring to late
  summer depending on the
  warmth as they go when it
  gets cold); gurnard (a firm
  fish); lemon sole (around
  most of the year); scallops
  (a Christmas treat through
  to April); red mullet (available
  July to November); plaice
  (March to December); sea
  bass (July to December)

1 Ask the fishmonger to fillet the fish for you and at home cut it into pieces about 5cm x 3cm.

2 Sweat the onion, carrot, celery and fennel in the olive oil without colouring them. Add the garlic and tomato purée. Add the white wine and reduce a little. Add the saffron, bay leaf and fish stock. Bring to the boil, then simmer for 20 minutes. Adjust the seasoning.

3 Put the fish and shellfish into a pan and cover with the soup base. Bring to the boil, then simmer for a few minutes, until the fish is cooked through. Discard any shellfish that don't open. Finish with a knob of butter and some chopped flat-leaf parsley.

ROASTED SEA BASS AND FENNEL (SPIGOLA AL FINOCCHIO)

ALDO ZILLI, CHEF PATRON, ZILLI FISH, LONDON

'You can cook bass in so many ways – you can even have it raw, when it is very fresh, thinly sliced and dressed with a little soy sauce, lemon juice and coriander,' writes Aldo Zilli. 'Fennel is one of my favourite vegetables and sea bass is definitely my favourite fish, so this, for me, is a marriage made in heaven.'

serves 6

2 baking potatoes, peeled and
   sliced 1cm thick
1.4kg whole sea bass, scaled
   and gutted
2–4 rosemary sprigs
2 cloves of garlic, peeled and
   sliced
½ lemon, thinly sliced
6 tbsp olive oil
sea salt and freshly ground
   black pepper
20g fennel seeds
2 medium fennel bulbs

1 Parboil the sliced potatoes for 2 minutes and drain.

2 Make several diagonal incisions across each side of the fish, making sure you don't go through to the bone. Wash and dry.

3 Place a small sprig of rosemary and a slice of garlic in each slit, and put the remaining garlic and rosemary into the gut of the fish with the lemon slices.

4 Rub the fish with 4 tbsp olive oil and sprinkle with sea salt, half the fennel seeds and pepper.

5 Slice the fresh fennel lengthways into 1cm thick pieces. Place the potato and fennel in a baking tray and sprinkle with the remaining fennel seeds, salt and pepper. Place the fish on top and drizzle with 2 tbsp olive oil.

6 Preheat the oven to 190°C/375°F/gas mark 5. Cover the tray with foil and cook for about 35 minutes. The fish is cooked when the flesh is opaque even at the thickest point.

7 Serve on a plate with the potato and fennel set around the fish and garnished with a sprig of rosemary.

SALMON WITH PANCETTA (INVOLTINI DI SALMONE)

ALDO ZILLI, CHEF-PATRON, ZILLI FISH, LONDON

'I didn't cook salmon or smoked salmon until I came to the UK, but my love for this wonderful fish came when I worked in a hotel in London. The chef was Scottish, so many recipes involved salmon and smoked salmon. I remember one day he roasted a whole side of smoked salmon with some cracked pepper on top. What a result! I still serve it every now and then in the restaurants,' writes Aldo Zilli. This recipe uses fresh salmon.

serves 4

800g fresh salmon fillet
8 slices Italian pancetta, thinly sliced
350g fresh leaf spinach, stalks removed
2 tbsp olive oil, plus extra for drizzling
freshly ground black pepper
25g butter
1 clove of garlic, peeled and finely chopped

1 Slice the salmon fillet into four equal portions, about 200g each. Make sure all the fish bones are removed. Wrap two slices of pancetta around each piece of salmon. Wrap each piece of salmon in cling film and refrigerate for half an hour.

2 Preheat the oven to 200°C/400°F/gas mark 6.

3 Wash and drain the spinach.

4 Put some 2 tbsp olive oil in an ovenproof, shallow, non-stick pan over a medium heat. Season the salmon with pepper and cook presentation-side down in the pan for 2 minutes, then place in a roasting tin in the oven for 4 minutes.

5 While the fish is cooking, melt the butter in another shallow pan. Cook the spinach and garlic in the butter on a medium heat and then season. Remove from the heat after 1 minute and the spinach will wilt naturally. Drain the spinach on kitchen paper and place in the middle of a plate, then place the salmon on top, drizzle with olive oil and serve.

HAKE IN CHERRY TOMATO AND WINE BROTH (NASELLO IN GUAZZETTO)

ALDO ZILLI, CHEF-PATRON, ZILLI FISH, LONDON

'This fish dish was one of the first recipes I made when I was a junior in a hotel in the Adriatic coast,' writes Zilli. 'It was extremely popular because the hake was caught just off shore so it was always lovely and fresh. The fish was on the menu served with many different sauces, but this was the best combination as far as I was concerned: simple and very tasty.'

serves 4

4 tbsp extra-virgin olive oil
1 small red onion, peeled and finely diced
1 clove of garlic, peeled and crushed
1 rosemary sprig
4 x 200g hake fillets
salt and freshly ground black pepper
1 carrot, peeled and finely diced
2 celery sticks, trimmed and finely diced
350g cherry tomatoes, halved
100ml dry white wine
450ml fish stock
3 tbsp fresh thyme leaves
8 fresh sage leaves, finely chopped

1 Preheat the oven to 200°C/400°F/gas mark 6. Put 2 tbsp olive oil in a large ovenproof pan and place over a low heat. Add the onion, garlic and rosemary and sauté for 5–6 minutes, until soft.

2 Cut the fish fillets in half. Season the fish with salt and pepper. Add the fish to the onion mixture and cook for 3–4 minutes, turning the fish several times.

3 Gently stir in the remaining vegetables, tomato and wine. Simmer for 5 minutes to reduce the wine. Add the stock and remaining herbs and bring to the boil.

4 Transfer the fish and vegetables to the oven for 15 minutes, or until the fish is cooked through. For a light lunch, spoon the fish and vegetables into the centre of four shallow bowls, then gently spoon over the broth. Drizzle over the remaining olive oil and serve.

POACHED OYSTERS WITH SMOKED SALMON, CUCUMBER AND CHIVES

ROWLEY LEIGH, CHEF-PATRON AND FISH-SHOP OWNER, KENSINGTON PLACE, LONDON

Rowley Leigh wanted Kensington Place to be an English version of the French brasserie, and took the chance to open a fish shop at the side of the restaurant, rather as the French display rows of briny oysters. The Kensington Place Fish Shop treats fish with respect. Just one or a few specimens of each species are displayed on the ice, where you can gaze at a perfect turbot or some silver-bright herrings. Some fillets are kept carefully in chilled drawers below the slab and the rest of the fish are kept whole in a walk-in refrigerator. Chefs work here both preparing the fish and cooking dishes, such as fish soup and seared tuna with ginger and soy sauce. The manager, Colin Westal, gets up at 2.30a.m. in order to get to Billingsate early to snap up the pick of the catch.

serves 4 as a starter

20 rock oysters
150g sliced smoked salmon
1 cucumber
100g unsalted butter
50ml double cream
freshly ground black pepper
1 handful of chopped fresh chives

1 Open the oysters, reserving the liquor and removing the meat. Rinse the rounded halves of the shells and put them on a large serving dish in a warm oven.

2 Cut the smoked salmon into very thin strips. Cut the cucumber flesh into matchsticks.

3 Melt a small knob of the butter in a frying pan and quickly toss the cucumber in it. Remove from the heat and put the smoked salmon in the pan, tossing the two together very briefly to mix but without cooking the salmon. Put a small bundle of the mixture in each shell.

4 Put the oyster liquor in a wide, shallow saucepan. Bring to the boil. Turn down the heat, put the oysters in and simmer for less than a minute. Remove the oysters and put one in each of the rounded half-shells. Bring the liquid back to the boil and reduce down to about 2 tbsp. Add the cream and reduce until the sauce starts to thicken.

5 Cut the rest of the butter into cubes (it has to be quite cold: if the butter melts too fast the sauce could separate), and whisk into the sauce. Add plenty of black pepper to the emulsified sauce and spoon over each oyster. Sprinkle over lots of chopped chives and serve as a luxurious starter.

OPENING OYSTERS Use a sturdy oyster knife, preferably one with a guard. Fold a kitchen cloth into a thick square and place in the left hand. Secure the oyster in the cloth with the flat side of the shell uppermost and the hinged, thicker end towards you. Push the oyster knife at a 45-degree angle in at the hinge: the knife will penetrate easily if you are in the right place. Rotate the knife a quarter turn back and forth, increasing pressure as you do so, until, with a little plop, the pressure is released and the oyster opens. Slide the knife along the top of the oyster and remove the top shell. If cooking the oyster, slip the knife under it and cut the muscle. Collect them in a small bowl in their juice. Covered in cling film and well refrigerated, they will keep for a day or two in this condition.

EAST ANGLIA

With the exception of Lowestoft, East Anglia has long been a coastline of small fishing fleets. Numbers in most places have dwindled to the few, but you can still find stalls and shops selling fresh local fish near the sea where it was caught. Both the chefs and home cooks of the area value their food producers, and a strong sense of regional food pervades here. Look out for specialities such as the Stiffkey blue cockles, the summer sea bass,

'YOU CAN STILL FIND STALLS AND LOCAL SHOPS SELLING FRESH LOCAL FISH NEAR THE SEA WHERE IT WAS CAUGHT.'

the brown shrimps from the Wash and the famous Cromer crabs.

Herring made the name of Lowestoft, and there are some exceptional smoke houses in the region smoking kippers, bloaters and red herring. They may, these days, import their fish to get a bigger size. Meanwhile, the rivers Blackwater and Thames now have an accredited sustainable herring fishery from the autumn to the spring, and the Essex native oyster fishery has also been revived.

BROKEN SALMON, CUCUMBER AND LETTUCE SALAD WITH FRESH DILL CREAM DRESSING

GARY RHODES, CHEF, RHODES TWENTY FOUR, LONDON

'Although prepared indoors, this is most certainly a dish for the garden', writes Gary Rhodes. 'Few of our home-grown delights need playing with or garnishing during the three peak summer months. Fresh salmon can be poached and served cold, or lightly steamed — as here. And during these summer months, cucumber finds a new identity, its watery flesh offering a more pronounced flavour.

'This dish is simply a combination of the two main ingredients tossed amongst gentle leaves, which are sweet, not too bitter and overpowering, finished with a creamy dill dressing. To bulk up the salad, broken steamed or boiled potatoes can be added, or served just rolled in butter and sitting in a bowl alongside.'

serves 4

1 small Butterhead or loose-leaf lettuce
1 small Cos lettuce
1 Little Gem lettuce
a handful of baby spinach or purslane leaves
½ cucumber
knob of butter, plus more for greasing
coarse sea salt and freshly ground black pepper

450g salmon fillet, skinned and pin-boned

for the dressing
2 tbsp natural yogurt
3 tbsp single cream
juice of 1 lime, or 1–2 tbsp white wine vinegar
2 tbsp olive oil
1 tbsp chopped fresh dill

1 Remove any damaged leaves from the lettuce before tearing the leaves from the base stalk. Gently rinse under cold water along with the spinach or sprigs of purslane. Leave to drain in a large colander or spin in a wire salad basket.

2 Split the cucumber in half lengthwise, dividing each half into three or four long wedges. Slice each wedge into 5mm thick pieces.

3 To steam the salmon, butter a sheet of greaseproof paper, seasoning with the sea salt and pepper. Place the salmon on one half of the paper, skinned-side down, top with a knob of butter and sprinkle with a little sea salt.

4 Fold the paper over the fish, and place in a steamer basket or colander over a saucepan of rapidly simmering water. Cover with a lid and steam for 8–10 minutes. (A thin fillet of salmon may take only 6 minutes to steam.) This will leave a pink centre with a succulent bite. To check, lift the folded greaseproof paper. The salmon should be slightly opaque, still showing signs of its natural pink. If it is too soft to the touch, continue to steam for a few minutes more until it is just beginning to firm. Once it is at this stage, remove the basket from the pan and leave to one side.

5 While steaming the fish, spoon the yogurt, single cream and lime juice or vinegar together, whisking in the olive oil. Season with salt and pepper and add the chopped dill.

6 Tear the salad leaves and mix with the cucumber in a large bowl. Using a fish slice, transfer the steamed salmon on to a plate and break it into bite-size pieces with a fork. Whisk any juice left on the greaseproof into the dressing.

7 Add the salmon to the leaves, pouring the dressing over. Gently spoon all the flavours together in a rustic fashion, serving as it is or in individual portions.

STEAMED HALIBUT AND CABBAGE WITH A SALMON GRAVADLAX SAUCE

GARY RHODES, CHEF, RHODES TWENTY FOUR, LONDON

'In the 19th century, halibut wasn't thought much of in England, but it's certainly appreciated now,' writes Gary Rhodes. 'The largest of the flat fish, it is increasingly rare from the wild, but is now being farmed. This is quite a basic recipe — steamed fish served with buttered cabbage — which sounds, and is, very British in concept. But I have added a few details just to lift it a little out of the ordinary, with a salmon gravadlax sauce and sesame seeds to go with the accompanying cabbage. This is a classic instance of how to bring basic flavours up to date. There are quite a few components to this recipe, but all it needs is planning ahead. All of the flavours work so well together, with the lemon oil lifting and marrying them all.'

serves 4

for the salmon gravadlax
15g coarse sea salt
15g caster sugar
freshly ground black pepper
splash of brandy
450g salmon fillet, skinned and pin-boned

for the sauce
butter
2 tbsp finely chopped shallots
2–3 tbsp brandy
1 tsp demerara sugar
3 tbsp white wine
2 tsp white wine vinegar
150ml fish stock
150ml double cream
2–3 tsp Dijon mustard
1 tsp chopped fresh dill

4 x 175–225g halibut fillet portions
salt and freshly ground black pepper
butter, plus extra for greasing
1 small Savoy cabbage, finely shredded
1–2 tsp sesame seeds, toasted
4 tbsp olive oil
1 tbsp lemon juice

1 For the salmon gravadlax, mix together the coarse sea salt, sugar and pepper and moisten with the brandy. Spread over the salmon fillet before cling filming and allow to cure for 6 hours in a cold place such as a refrigerator.

2 Cut the salmon into 5mm dice for the garnish. You will probably need no more than 100–150g. It's best to cure 450g as a minimum to achieve the best results; the rest can be thinly sliced and enjoyed with a squeeze of lemon.

3 To make the sauce, melt a small knob of butter in a saucepan. Cook the shallot for a few minutes without colouring. Add the brandy and demerara sugar and allow to boil and reduce until you have a syrupy consistency.

4 Add the white wine and white wine vinegar and reduce to the same stage. Pour in the fish stock and boil until reduced by half. Add the double cream along with the Dijon mustard. Season with salt and bring to a simmer.

5 Season the halibut with salt and pepper. Sit on buttered paper and steam above boiling water for 8–10 minutes.

6 While steaming, melt a knob of butter in a large pan and add the cabbage. Stir well and add 1–2 tbsp water. This will create steam and cook the cabbage within a few minutes. Season and add the toasted sesame seeds.

7 Mix together the olive oil and lemon juice and season with salt and pepper.

8 Divide the cabbage between four plates, sitting the halibut on top. Add the diced gravadlax to the sauce, along with the chopped dill, and spoon over.

9 Drizzle the lemony olive oil over the halibut and around the dish.

PAN-FRIED SEA BASS WITH BLACKBERRY SHALLOTS AND CREAMY HOLLANDAISE SAUCE

GARY RHODES, CHEF, RHODES TWENTY FOUR, LONDON

'Sea bass has the advantage of being available all year round, and an extra bonus is that it has few bones,' writes Gary Rhodes. 'Over the years, it has become highly prized — the "caviar" of round fish. Before filleting, please ask the fishmonger for the fish to be scaled; this prevents the flesh from becoming damaged and leaves a neater finish. The blackberry flavour to the shallots — which are a perfect accompaniment to the fine flavour of sea bass — is not due to the fruit itself, but to the French blackberry liqueur crème de mûre. This fish recipe is best as a starter or fish course. If it were to be served as a main course, Jersey Royals and English spinach would eat well as accompaniments.'

serves 4

4 x 100–175g sea bass fillet portions, scaled and skin on
30g butter
450g large shallots, peeled and cut into rings
2 glasses of red wine
2 tsp demerara sugar
2–3 tbsp crème de mure (crème de cassis, the blackcurrant variety, can also be used)
flour, for dusting
1 tbsp cooking oil
salt and freshly ground black pepper

for the creamy hollandaise sauce
1 quantity simple hollandaise sauce (see page 74)
100ml double cream (150ml can be used for a creamier finish)

1 Start to soften the shallot in half the butter for 2–3 minutes. Add the red wine and 1 tsp sugar. The heat can now be increased to create a gentle bubble to braise the shallot. Once the wine has reduced to three-quarters, add the crème de mûre, allowing it to reduce lightly. If the flavour is over-sharp, add the remaining teaspoon of sugar. The shallots are best left now to cool and marinate in the cooking syrup for a few hours. (If left overnight, the flavour becomes even more intense.)

2 Season the sea bass fillets with salt and pepper and lightly flour the skin. Smear the remaining half of the butter on each floured side.

3 Heat 1 tbsp cooking oil in a frying pan. Place the fillets, skin-side down, in the pan. Cook on a medium heat without shaking the pan, allowing the butter to melt and bubble along with the flour, creating a crisp finish. Cook for 4–5 minutes before turning and frying for a further 2 minutes.

4 While pan-frying the fish, reheat the shallots.

5 If serving the creamy hollandaise sauce, lightly whip the double cream and gently fold into the simple hollandaise. The sauce is now ready to offer, providing a soft, creamy balance to the richness of the complete dish.

6 To serve, spoon the shallots into the centre of four plates, trickling the rich syrup around. Place the crisp sea bass fillets on top.

HOLLANDAISE SAUCE

GARY RHODES, CHEF, RHODES TWENTY FOUR, LONDON

'I'm not sure how this famous butter sauce found its name, but it certainly wasn't from Holland,' writes Gary Rhodes. 'It's a French classic, and has also been known as a sauce Isigny, named after the home town of France's finest butter. Classically, a white-wine vinegar reduction is made, similar to that in Béarnaise sauce, but without the herbs. In this simple version, acidity is provided by lemon juice, which also lends its wonderful fruit flavour.'

makes about 200ml

175g unsalted butter
2 egg yolks

2 tbsp warm water
juice of 1 lemon
salt and cayenne or
    ground white pepper

1 Clarify the butter by heating it until its solids separate from the rich yellow oil. Remove from the heat and leave to cool until just warm. The solids will now be at the base of the pan. Any excess solids on top can be skimmed away.

2 Add the yolks to the water with half the lemon juice. Whisk over a pan of simmering water to a ribbon stage, until at least doubled in volume, lighter in colour, and almost the consistency of softly whipped cream.

3 Remove from the heat and slowly add the clarified butter, whisking vigorously. This will emulsify the butter into the egg yolk mixture. If the sauce seems too thick and almost sticky while adding the butter, loosen slightly with another squeeze of lemon juice or water.

4 Season with salt and cayenne or white pepper, and add the remaining lemon juice, if needed, to enrich the total flavour. The sauce is now ready to serve. For a guaranteed smooth, silky finish, once seasoned, strain through a sieve. Keep the sauce in a warm bowl and cover with cling film for up to 1 hour before use. If allowed to cool, the butter sets and the sauce separates when reheated, so don't let this happen.

Hollandaise sauce can take on a lot more flavours, so here are a few suggestions:

· For a sauce mousseline add whipped cream before serving.

· Add 1–2 tsp Dijon mustard for sauce moutarde.

· Melt the butter to a nut-brown stage before adding; this gives you a sauce noisette.

· Replace the lemon juice with the juice of 2–3 blood oranges, reduced to a syrupy consistency: the finely grated zest of 1 unwaxed blood orange can be added to the boiling juices to tenderize. When added to a basic hollandaise, this creates a classic sauce maltaise, perfect for serving with grilled duck, game or fish dishes.

GIGOT OF COD

ANDREW CLARKE, MOBILE FISHMONGER BASED IN LOWESTOFT, SUFFOLK

Andrew Clarke buys fish from Lowestoft market and sells it from a converted coach in markets around London and the South-East. He says line-caught cod from this part of the coast is a stunning fish, and for this dish he uses as big a piece of cod as he can get hold of from the thick, loin end down towards the tail. This is the most expensive part of the fish, and you may be charged a premium for it, but it's worth every penny for its large, juicy flakes of fish. Sometimes you can find a single 900g loin; otherwise, use two smaller ones. The best time for Lowestoft cod is when there is colder water, from October to May.

serves 4

700–900g cod loin
2–4 small cloves of garlic, peeled
olive oil
salt and freshly ground black pepper
handful of herbs, such as basil, fennel tops, dill – whatever you want

1 Preheat the oven to 200°C/400°F/gas mark 6.

2 Crush the garlic cloves roughly with the blade of a big knife, so they stay in one piece. Fry them quickly in 1 tsp olive oil to brown slightly.

3 Make a couple of small slits in the cod loin and push the garlic into them.

4 Put the cod on a piece of foil large enough to wrap up the fish. Pour over a good slosh of olive oil and season with salt and pepper. Scatter some roughly torn or chopped herbs around the fish. Seal the foil parcel.

5 Cook in the hot oven for 20–25 minutes. Two smaller loins will take a little less time to cook than a single large one.

6 When the fish is cooked, bring the foil parcel to the table and open it up so the aromas of the cod, garlic and herbs come out when you open it. Serve with a fresh seasonal vegetable and mashed potato.

TOP, LEFT TO RIGHT
Former fisherman Richard
Davis and his fisherman son
John sell shellfish at their
family's shop in Cromer;
scrubbing and boiling Cromer
crabs; Cromer crabs, which
are small and sweet fleshed;
Mac's, one of the small
independent fish shops where
you can eat Norfolk seafood.
BELOW Crabs being lifted out
of the boiler.

CRABBING

A 40-mile stretch of the Norfolk coast produces the celebrated Cromer crab. In a convenient, natural portion, each sweet, compact crab feeds one person. All over Cromer's Victorian seaside streets are stalls of shellfish. Some shops have the prices painted on pebbles next to the seafood; many advertise themselves as fishermen/sellers on chalked-up boards.

One of the most well known of these shops is run by the Davis family, and their operation epitomises the best sort of local loop between sea and shellfish feast. Beyond Cromer's elegant cast-iron pier, 10 sturdy crabbing boats sit on the beach ready to go. John Davis was three when he first went to sea in one such vessel. Over the years, his father Richard taught him longshore fishing — which has earned the family a living for at least eight generations — catching whatever swims or scuttles within a few miles of the land, be it herring in autumn, white fish in winter or crabs and lobsters in summer. Supply and demand have both changed, and now John mostly goes out before dawn at all times of year with long strings of pots to catch crustacea.

The trick to catching the local speciality, John says, is 'to think like a crab,' understanding how they feed and the patterns of the sea. Crabs are tempted into pots with fresh fish, generally what is left once the plaice and cod fillets have been sold. Lobsters go for oilier bait, such as mackerel. The fast and fierce big-clawed lobster also attacks and eats crabs, especially if it needs to build up its shell after moulting. A crab tends to steer clear of a pot if it contains a lobster.

Crab and lobster potting is highly selective. Undersized crabs and females with eggs are returned to the sea to breed and grow. In the summer breeding months, John can put back as many as 40 crabs to every one landed.

As well as learning his trade from his father and grandfather, John learned from the first crew member on his boat, 'Teapot' West. Fishermen nicknames come about partly because so many have the same name. At one time, neighbouring Sheringham had 13 fishing Mr Wests (five of them Henrys), so they gave them all nicknames: Downtide, Joyful, Doker, Teapot, Fiddy, Raleigh, Jacko, Paris, Oden, Squinter, Nuts, Custard and Tweet.

Back ashore, John and his crew take the crabs to a converted stable in Cromer, near the family shop. Amidst plumes of steam, they cook their catch for 15-20 minutes in cauldrons, then the shellfish are washed down and cooled. Spare crabpots are piled up outside, the markers on the attached buoys (pieces of old sack tied around posts) fluttering like plastic butterflies amidst the cobbles.

The crab's next stop is the picking room. John's mother, Julie, in her youth thought she would run a dress shop. Then she married into fishing. Dressing a crab is at least as meticulous a task as sewing a garment. Two workers deal with 500-600 crustacea a day. A practised picker sorts a crab in 29 moves, flicking and scooping out shards of pearly white flesh from the inner structure and claws, extracting every last gram with the end of a teaspoon and a knife. A good worker can do an astonishing 40-50 in an hour.

The crab's shell acts as a ready-made plate, with the white meat piled at one end and the paste of brown meat at the other (although it is called brown meat, it takes on different hues depending on the creature's feed).

Then the shellfish go to the shop, right by the picking room. Cromer crabs are best fresh from the pot. The Davises sell that morning's catch in the shop that very day. If no crabs are caught, none are sold. Less expert retailers often sell these shellfish defrosted; you can spot such crabs because claws have meat tinged orange when fresh and are more reddish when they have come out of a freezer.

The best times of year for catching crabs are spring and early summer, from March to June, and at the end of October and November, when they have moulted and are feeding hard to keep going until winter. Others put their prices up and down according to supplies, but the Davises have kept theirs the same for years, starting at £1 a crab.

The number of crabs caught seems to be holding up, as it is in many parts of the country. Some say this is because there are fewer fish competing for food.

Just as John Davis fishes mostly for crustacea these days, economics have made another change to the Cromer fleet. Most of the boats are now single-handed, despite the well-known dangers of this stretch of coast.

GOUJONS OF DOVER SOLE

THANE PRINCE, FOOD WRITER AND COOKERY SCHOOL OWNER, ALDEBURGH

Thane Prince and Sara Fox at the Aldeburgh Cookery School believe in the importance of good ingredients and take people on their courses to meet Dean Fryer, who sells his freshly caught fish from his baiting shed on the beach. Between the end of May and the beginning of November he lands Dover sole, going out in the early hours of the morning and landing between 5a.m. and 10a.m. In the winter, he baits lines with sprats or squid, and catches cod, skate, dogfish and the odd sea bass. When he started 20 years ago, there were 25 boats on the beach; now he is one of only three full-time fishermen left. He says the people on the cookery courses, who make this dish at the school, are amazed by the freshness of the fish and the fact that there are still people working on this small scale, landing and selling local fish in prime condition.

serves 4

2–3 skinless Dover sole fillets per person
4 tbsp plain flour seasoned with salt and white pepper
2 eggs, beaten with a good pinch of salt
110g fresh white breadcrumbs
oil, for deep-frying

1 Cut the sole fillets into long, thin strips and dust lightly with seasoned flour.

2 Dip into the egg mixture and then roll in breadcrumbs.

3 Place the goujons, well spaced, on a sheet of non-stick or greaseproof paper. Cover and refrigerate until needed.

4 Heat the oil to medium, so a cube of bread will brown in 30 seconds. Fry the goujons a few at a time until browned, then drain on kitchen paper. Serve with tartare sauce.

CRAB DIP

JULIE DAVIS, CRAB SELLER FROM A FISHING FAMILY, CROMER, NORFOLK

Julie Davis sells her son John's crabs from the family shop in Garden Street in Cromer. Whenever she goes to a function, she is asked to bring along her famous crab dip. Made in minutes, it is a quick and easy starter. The whole crab is used, with the brown meat providing lots of flavour and the white meat offering sweet succulence.

serves 4 as a starter

2 medium dressed Cromer crabs (225–300g each) or 1 large dressed crab from elsewhere
2 spring onions, all the white and a bit of the green, chopped
¼–½ tsp mustard powder, to taste

sprinkle of cayenne pepper
freshly ground black pepper
a couple of drops of Worcestershire sauce
small pinch of garlic salt
squeeze of lemon juice
2–3 tbsp crème fraîche (or a mixture of mayonnaise and double cream)

1 Mix the meat from the crabs with all the other ingredients, adding enough cream to get a consistency that will work as a dip.

2 Serve the crab dip with savoury biscuits, crisps and vegetables such as short sticks of celery, carrots and cucumber.

ITALIAN BBQ FISH

ANDREW COOK, CHEF, FRUITS OF THE SEA, BLAKENEY, NORFOLK

Enterprising fisherman Willie Weston has set up a fish shop and seafood café, Fruits of the Sea, in Blakeney on the North Norfolk coast. His wife Dawn and his chef Andrew Cook have devised ways to prepare the local seafood so that people can either eat it in the café or take it away to cook at home. This is one of their recipes that can be cooked on a barbecue or in the oven.

serves 4

1 Spanish onion, peeled and diced
4 slices smoked bacon, roughly chopped
2 tsp fennel seeds
1 tbsp olive oil
50g demerara sugar
300ml tomato passata
150ml HP brown sauce
salt and freshly ground black pepper
4 sea bass (450–500g each) or 4 mackerel, gutted and trimmed

1 Preheat the oven to 220°C/425°F/gas mark 7. Put the onion, bacon and fennel seeds in an ovenproof dish and stir with the olive oil.

2 Put in the oven for 20 minutes so the onion just starts to caramelize a little on top. Stir in the sugar and cook, still uncovered, for another 20 minutes.

3 Stir in the passata and brown sauce. Cook uncovered in the oven for another 20 minutes. Season with salt and pepper. If you are not cooking the fish straight away, allow the sauce to cool.

4 Put the fish on four rectangles of foil, big enough to enclose it. Make three slashes on both sides of each fish and cover with the sauce. Close up the foil to make trim parcels. You can do this a day in advance if the fish are really fresh, and leave the fish in the refrigerator until you are ready to cook them.

5 Cook the foil parcels in the preheated oven or on a barbecue for 20–30 minutes, or until cooked. Check after 20 minutes and give them longer if they need it.

6 You could serve this, perhaps, with sautéed rosemary potatoes and Waldorf salad.

COCKLE CHOWDER

GALTON BLAKISTON, CHEF-PATRON, MORSTON HALL, MORSTON, NORFOLK

Galton Blakiston spent his childhood summer holidays on the north Norfolk coast, near where he and his wife Tracy now run their Michelin-starred hotel and restaurant, Morston Hall. His family holidays were spent shrimping, spearing flat fish, catching mackerel using lines fluttering with feathers or milk-bottle tops, gathering samphire and raking up the sort of cockles that he now uses in this recipe. Every week he orders three bags of cockles from John-the-fish-man, who runs the North Norfolk Fish Company in Holt. This part of the world is so much part of the sea that Holt, a small market town with a population of around 5,000, has no fewer than four fishmongers.

serves 4

1kg cockles in shells, soaked in fresh cold water with a sprinkling of plain flour and kept in the refrigerator
2 tbsp olive oil
2 large banana shallots, peeled and thinly sliced
2 cloves of garlic, peeled and finely chopped
175ml dry white wine

275ml single cream
25g unsalted butter
2 red chillies, deseeded and finely chopped
1 small lobe of fresh ginger (about 5cm long), peeled and finely grated
2 tbsp chopped flat-leaf parsley
2 tbsp chopped chives
freshly ground black pepper

1 Drain the cockles in a colander and leave them under cold running water for a few minutes to get rid of the flour. Heat a large pan, add the oil, then the shallot and garlic, and sweat until they are just starting to colour.

2 Have the cockles ready and in one swoop add them to the shallot and garlic. Shake the pan, add the white wine, put a lid on and cook on a high heat until the cockles open. Take off the heat, allow to cool a little, then take the cockles from the shells (leaving a few in their shells if you prefer to see them in the dish). Discard any that have not opened – do not risk eating any!

3 Pour the liquor through a muslin-lined sieve into a bowl and reserve. Keep the cockles to one side.

4 To bring the soup together, heat the reserved liquor and reduce slightly over a high heat. Add the cream and reduce again until it has slightly thickened. Five minutes before serving, add the cockles and turn the heat down. Just prior to serving, add the butter, stirring well, then the chilli and ginger, and lastly the parsley and chives. Season with a good grinding of pepper. Serve straight away with crusty bread.

WALES

Wales has a floating cottage industry of small vessels going out from ports, the numbers swelling in the summer when the weather calms and more diners are after a nice plate of seafood. Look out for the wild sea bass caught off such rocky shores as the Gower peninsula, and the plaice, skate, turbot, Dover sole, mackerel and lobster landed by these inshore boats. Mussels are a famous product of Conwy and are now also cultivated off Anglesey, alongside oysters.

Whelks have become one of the most commercial catches from Anglesea, to be exported to Korea, where they are eaten pickled as bar snacks. One of Wales' most celebrated specialities is sewin, or sea trout, caught commercially by licensed fishermen in the season from 1 April to the end of July, with some variation according to local by-laws. Some of the freshwater ones are even still caught in coracles.

'LOOK OUT FOR THE WILD SEA BASS CAUGHT OFF SUCH ROCKY SHORES AS THE GOWER PENINSULA.'

SALT-BAKED SEA BASS

LA BRASERIA, SWANSEA

This bustling bodega is a slice of Spanish dining in the centre of Swansea. A large display of raw fresh fish, bought daily, is on show in the upstairs dining room. You pick out what you want and it is cooked simply, to perfection. Salt-baking is one method they use for sea bass, including the wild ones caught off the rocks by Rhossili Bay on the Gower peninsula. The fish is cooked within a hard crust of salt so it bakes in its own juices, with succulent results. The restaurant uses the same method for the local sewin (or sea trout).

serves 4

4 x 550g sea bass (wild or farmed), scaled and gutted
coarse sea salt
lemon wedges, to serve

1 Preheat the oven to 240°C/475°F/gas mark 9.

2 Place the fish on a baking tray.

3 Moisten plenty of salt. It needs to be roughly the same texture as sand that is damp after the tide has run out; you want the salt to stick together, but not become runny.

4 Cover the exposed side of each of the fish with about 1cm of salt, from the gills to the base of the tail.

5 Cook in the oven for 25 minutes.

6 Crack open the hard rock-salt crust and peel it away carefully. Serve the fillets with a wedge of lemon, tartare sauce and baked potatoes or chips.

SOME WELSH WAYS WITH MUSSELS AND LAVER

GARETH WYNN JONES, LAVER GATHERER, GWYNEDD

Gareth Wynn Jones collects laver from the north Welsh coast and goes through the long, laborious process of washing it, boiling it in seawater, chopping and puréeing it, and boiling it down again to get what he prefers to call laver or laver purée rather than laverbread. He loves it as a vegetable in its own right and as an accompaniment to seafood. It goes particularly well with shellfish, including the excellent mussels from this part of the world — he just spreads laver on mussels and grills them — and it has an affinity with orange juice for a sauce to partner chicken or Welsh lamb, or in tartlets with wild mushrooms. Here he gives another recipe, using garlic and cream, plus an ultra-simple idea for a convenient supper that he cooks up when hungry and in a hurry after a day out. You can buy fresh or tinned laverbread.

mussels with cream

serves 4

30 large mussels, scrubbed and
  beards removed
½ bulb of garlic (or less),
  divided into cloves and
  peeled
300ml double cream
freshly ground black pepper
1 large handful of chopped
  fresh parsley, curly or
  flat-leaf (optional)

1 Crush the garlic cloves and put with the cream in a saucepan. Gently simmer for 5–10 minutes, making sure it doesn't boil. Turn off the heat and leave to infuse while you prepare the mussels.

2 Discard any mussels that are cracked or are open and don't close when tapped. Cook the mussels by putting them in a saucepan over a high heat. Cover with a lid for the first 30 seconds or so, then take off the lid so you can remove the mussels as they open. You are going to cook the meat further, so you do not want it to become chewy. Discard any mussels that don't open. Keep the juices for a shellfish risotto or suchlike.

3 Preheat the grill to high. Take the mussels out of the shells and put one into the larger half of each shell, discarding the rest of the shells. Spoon over the garlicky cream and grind over some black pepper. Put under the hot grill until the cream is bubbling and starting to brown.

4 If you like, scatter over some chopped parsley and serve with crusty bread and a salad.

fish fingers and laver

serves 2

8–12 high-quality fish fingers
6 tbsp warmed laver purée
½ lemon, cut into 2 wedges
chilled Champagne

1 Cook the fish fingers and serve with the warmed laver purée, lemon wedges and chilled Champagne.

CONWY PLAICE WITH A TOASTED NUT ROCKET PESTO

ROBERT CURETON, GASTROPUB OWNER, THE QUEEN'S HEAD, GLANWYDDEN, CONWY

The plump Conwy plaice are in season from September until Christmas, and this is when Robert Cureton serves them at his pub, The Queen's Head. One of the pioneers of the gastropub revolution, Robert has long made a feature of the local seafood, naming its provenance on the 'specials' blackboard, be it Conwy skate, Anglesey oysters, local lobsters, or the big Conwy mussels that he bakes with Llanrwst Cheddar in an award-winning dish. If a fish is in season, he serves it, then moves on to the next ones as they reach their peak.

serves 4

4 large Conwy plaice fillets
  (225–275g each)
seasoned plain flour
butter, for greasing
450g fresh leaf spinach,
  washed
12 baby tomatoes, whole or
  halved

for the pesto
1 clove of garlic, peeled and
  chopped
2 good handfuls of rocket
handful of lightly toasted pine
  nuts, cooled
handful of grated Parmesan
extra-virgin olive oil

1 Preheat the oven to 200°C/400°F/gas mark 6.

2 To make the pesto, place the garlic and rocket in a food processor with the toasted pine nuts. Pulse until the mixture has been coarsely ground.

3 Turn out the mixture into a bowl and add half the Parmesan. Gently stir in enough olive oil to bind: the consistency should be firm but semi-wet. Season to taste and add the rest of the Parmesan.

4 Dip the plaice fillets in seasoned flour and bake them on a buttered tray in the oven for 5–10 minutes.

5 Quickly wilt the spinach by putting it in a large covered pan over a medium heat, turning it over once or twice.

6 To serve, put the wilted spinach and baby tomatoes on four plates, place the fish on top and spoon on the pesto.

THAI FISH CAKES

PAVINEE TARUSCHIO, MOBILE CATERER, PAV'S KITCHEN

Pavinee, the daughter of Franco and Ann Taruschio, who used to run the renowned gastropub The Walnut Tree in Abergavenny, is continuing the family's fine culinary tradition. She takes her mobile catering outfit, Pav's Kitchen, to events such as the spirited Abergavenny Food Festival, and from it she serves dishes such as these fish cakes. This recipe uses a cheap alternative to cod – coley – or you could use any other white fish; even budget 'fish bits' from the fishmonger's trimmings.

makes 20; serves 4–5 as a starter

for the spice paste
5 dried red chillies, halved and deseeded
1 shallot, peeled and finely chopped
2 cloves of garlic, peeled and finely chopped
2 coriander roots or a small bunch of stems, finely chopped
6 fresh kaffir lime leaves, finely chopped, or 2 tsp finely grated lime zest
½ tsp salt
(or use 1 tbsp Thai red curry paste)

450g coley fillets, skinned and ground in a food processor
1 tbsp fish sauce
60g French beans, finely chopped
vegetable oil, for deep-frying

for the relish
125ml rice vinegar
2 tbsp white sugar
¼ cucumber, halved and thinly sliced
1 small carrot, halved and thinly sliced
3 shallots, peeled and finely sliced
1 medium chilli, deseeded and finely sliced
1 tbsp roughly ground roasted peanuts

1 To make the spice paste, grind the dried red chillies, shallot, garlic, coriander, lime leaves and salt to a fine paste in a spice grinder. Alternatively, just use 1 tbsp Thai red curry paste.

2 Add 1 tbsp of paste to the fish and thoroughly blend it together with your fingers.

3 Add the fish sauce and green beans and knead together. Make into 6cm small, flat cakes (about 1cm thick).

4 To make the relish, heat the vinegar with the sugar, stirring until the sugar dissolves, then boil for 5–6 minutes to get a thin syrup. Leave to cool.

5 When cold, add the cucumber, carrot, shallots and chilli and mix well. Top with the ground peanuts.

6 Deep-fry the fish cakes in moderately hot oil (190°C/375°F) so a cube of bread will fry in 40 seconds. Fry in batches and drain on kitchen paper. Serve with the relish.

COCKLE PICKING

Penclawdd, the cockle capital of South Wales, has long benefited from a sustainable fishery where the shellfish are picked by hand from the bed of the Burry Inlet. The 55 licensed pickers, many from local families who have gathered cockles for generations, follow the ebbing tide out to the extensive shellfish beds and return as the sea comes in again. The cocklers need to know the weather and the ways of the waters. Mist and rain can sweep in and obliterate their bearings, and the winds can hasten the returning tide.

The equipment for cockle gathering is simple: a knife known as a 'scrap' to scrape away the sand, a 'cram' to rake in the shellfish and a 'riddle' that sieves out the sand and undersized shells, ensuring only mature cockles are picked.

This back-breaking task is now done mostly by men, but the gathering used to be women's work, supplementing the men's income from mines and farms. The cocklers would ride donkeys, and then horses and carts, through the marshes and on to the sands to the 11,000 hectares of cockle beds. Tractors finally took over from horsepower only 15 years ago.

In the old days, women carried the shellfish on their heads, going to Swansea to shout of their wares on the streets. After the arrival of the railways in the 19th century, the 'cockle express' took their stock towards bigger markets, including America. The women would also use trains to drop off basketfuls at local stations, returning by foot to pick up and sell these salty nuggets of seaside freshness.

Most of the cockles are now exported, with Holland being the main buyer, followed by Spain and France, but there is also a strong local following. A circle of shellfish sellers forms the centre of Swansea city centre's busy indoor market, where shoppers of all ages buy small tubs of cockles, ready-to-eat with a sprinkle of pepper and a drop of vinegar, and perhaps also take away some green-black laver to fry up in bacon fat or heat in the microwave.

Cockle prices rose as the export market developed in the 1990s, and the fishery now makes a good living. But not all is plain sailing. After picking had to stop for a period due to concerns about a shellfish disease, there was a problem of underfishing. This was because when the fishery reopened the pickers naturally concentrated on gathering the super-big cockles. In the meantime, mild winters had led to a surge in spawn and beds became overcrowded because the cockles were not being thinned by picking. A lot died, showing how the beds must be harvested regularly.

The cockles start as tiny spat that drift and grow until size and gravity makes them settle in the sand, where they are soon the length of orange pips. The rich waters mean they grow so rapidly that they are ready to harvest in just 18 months. The shells take on the colours of the place where they lie, and in the past the dark-shelled cockles from silt used to go for boiling and shelling, while the lighter ones from the sands were sold in their shell.

Colour is now immaterial because most cockles are shelled. These waters are classified as grade 'B', not grade 'A', so the cockles would have to go through a purification plant to be sold live. It seems that, for the most part, there is not a big enough demand to justify this facility. Local cooks, therefore, miss out on the chance to rattle shells around a pan until the cockles open and give out their juices, making the magic in a cockle chowder or pasta sauce.

On an industrial estate in Crofty, just outside Penclawdd, dull road suddenly gives way to a gleaming expanse of cockle-shell gravel. This beautiful material is used on most of the paths of Gower Golf Club in Swansea, and it is laid down in gardens for the blind, who enjoy its crunch.

Beside the gravel is the Penclawdd Shellfish Processing Company. This started as a cooperative of 11 cockle families who got together to buy the equipment needed for modern health regulations. Here, the cockles are cooked, shelled, sorted and packaged. The company's MD, Mark Swistun, is the fifth generation of a cockle family. He remembers everyone pitching in during the cottage-industry days, when the shells were shovelled into vats steaming on fires in gardens along the estuary. People look out for each other, he says, in the face of the elements as they sift through the sands: 'The cockles have been of great value, and more than the money is the community value over the years.'

LEFT **Calm weather can quickly turn to mist and rain, so cocklers need to know their terrain in order to work safely.**

BAKED SEAFOOD WITH LAVERBREAD

FRANCO AND ANN TARUSCHIO, CHEF AND FOOD WRITER

Franco and Ann Taruschio used to take raw recruits at their former restaurant, The Walnut Tree Inn near Abergavenny in south Wales, to see the cockle picking in the Burry Inlet, so they would appreciate the hard work that went into their ingredients. For the same reason, they also took their staff mackerel fishing. 'A tremendous amount of laver is eaten in Wales,' they write. 'Generally the laver is made into what is called "laverbread", though because this is the seaweed boiled to a mush it is rather a misnomer. The laverbread is mixed with oatmeal and made into small cakes, then fried in bacon fat and eaten with bacon.'

serves 4

8 clams (palourdes) or cockles in their shells
sprinkle of fine oatmeal (optional)
4 scallops in their shells
24 mussels in their shells
8 razor clams in their shells
dry white wine
12 raw scampi (langoustines), shelled
salt and freshly ground black pepper
100g (3¾oz) smoked pancetta, finely chopped
4 tbsp extra-virgin olive oil
200g (7oz) day-old breadcrumbs
200g (7oz) laverbread
1 lemon, cut into 4 wedges

1 Scrub the clams or cockles and, if necessary, purge them by putting them in cold water with a sprinkling of fine oatmeal and leaving them in the refrigerator overnight.

2 Open the clams or cockles with a knife and remove the empty top shells. Discard any that are already open.

3 Open the scallops and remove the flesh. Remove the greyish beard around the scallops and the blackish sac. Rinse the scallops under cold water and dry them on kitchen paper. Scrub the concave half-shells and return the scallops to them.

4 Scrub the mussels well and remove any beards. Discard any mussels or razor clams that have cracked shells or shells that do not close when tapped.

5 Steam open the mussels and razor clams in a shallow pan over a brisk heat with a little white wine added. As soon as the shells open, remove and discard the empty half-shells. Discard any shells that do not open.

6 Chop the razor meat roughly and return to the half-shell.

7 Split the scampi in half lengthways and remove the dark intestinal vein. Put all the seafood on a large baking tray. Season lightly with salt and pepper.

8 Preheat the oven to 200°C/400°F/gas mark 6. Fry the pancetta in 2 tbsp olive oil until the fat runs. Stir the breadcrumbs into the pancetta and oil.

9 Coat each piece of seafood with laverbread using a teaspoon. Sprinkle the pancetta and breadcrumb mixture on top, then drizzle with the remaining olive oil.

10 Bake for 10 minutes in the hot oven or until golden on top. Serve hot with lemon wedges.

SPAGHETTI, SALMON OR SEWIN AND SAMPHIRE (SPAGHETTI ALLE ALGHE CON SALMONE)

FRANCO AND ANN TARUSCHIO, CHEF AND FOOD WRITER

'Samphire grows on the salt marshes in Wales,' write Ann and Franco Taruschio. 'It is wonderfully salty and succulent and has a taste of the sea. It is also good eaten raw, dressed with oil and lemon juice. Sewin (or sea-trout) can be used instead of salmon.'

serves 4

200g fresh samphire
240–360g spaghetti (about 60g per person)
2 shallots, peeled and finely chopped
1 clove of garlic, peeled and finely chopped
4 tbsp olive oil
30g butter

100ml dry white wine
juice of ½ lemon
salt and freshly ground black pepper
2 slices of salmon or sewin (sea-trout) fillet, weighing 400g in total, cut into 1cm dice
200g plum tomatoes, skinned, deseeded and diced

1 Clean the samphire carefully and thoroughly. Drop it into a saucepan of boiling water and blanch for 1 minute. Drain in a colander and set aside.

2 Cook the spaghetti in plenty of boiling salted water until al dente. Drain the spaghetti and tip it into a large, heated bowl.

3 In the meantime, fry the shallot and garlic in the olive oil and butter until light gold. Add the white wine and boil to reduce by half. Season with the lemon juice, salt (if needed) and pepper.

4 Add the salmon or sewin to the sauce and stir to mix, then immediately pour the sauce over the spaghetti and toss well together. Add the fresh tomato cubes and samphire and mix in, then serve at once.

POACHED USK WILD SALMON, SOUSED VEGETABLES AND SAFFRON HOLLANDAISE

MATT TEBBUTT, CHEF-PATRON, THE FOXHUNTER, NANT-Y-DERRY, MONMOUTHSHIRE

The best chefs use their craft to bring the freshness of a fish's flavours to the plate. Matt Tebbutt at The Foxhunter in Nantyderry, near Abergavenny, shows his pedigree in dishes such as Usk salmon with brown shrimps and a parsley and caper salad, and roast cod in an octopus stew made with paprika. The dish he has given to this book is made with the now rare local wild salmon – Matt says you could also use wild bass or halibut – and shows off the colour and texture of the fish against the slight crunch and acidity of the soused vegetables and the rich, yellow saffron hollandaise.

serves 4

4 x 225g salmon fillets, skinned
½ bottle of white wine
a few white peppercorns
1 star anise
a few coriander seeds
a couple of parsley stalks
2–3 slices of unwaxed lemon
2 bay leaves
200ml white wine vinegar
1 onion, peeled and sliced
3 carrots, finely sliced
3 sticks of celery, finely sliced
a few sprigs of fresh dill

1 Put the white wine in a saucepan with 1.7–2.3 litres of water and add the peppercorns, star anise, coriander seeds, parsley stalks, lemon slices, bay leaves and white wine vinegar. Simmer for 30 minutes.

2 Put the onion, carrot and celery in the liquid and simmer for 10–15 minutes until just tender. The vinegar will have soused (or pickled) the vegetables.

3 Plunge the salmon fillets into the simmering stock. Remove the pan from the heat and cover. Leave the fish to poach for 8–10 minutes. Remove the salmon from the pan and keep warm.

4 Place some of the soused vegetables on four plates with a small amount of the drained cooking liquor. Place the salmon fillets on top with some sprigs of dill. Spoon a generous amount of hollandaise over the fish, allowing the two sauces to mix together.

5 Serve with nothing more than freshly boiled new potatoes, butter and sea salt.

for the saffron hollandaise
1 large glass white wine (roughly 300ml)
100ml white wine vinegar
2 shallots, roughly chopped
1 bay leaf
3–4 whole white peppercorns
pinch of saffron
3 egg yolks
250g melted, unsalted butter, filtered through a clean J-cloth to remove the milk solids
squeeze of lemon juice

1 Reduce the wine and vinegar in a pan with the shallot, bay, peppercorns and saffron. When left with 2 tsp of liquid in the pan, pour it into a bowl in a bain-marie. Whisk the yolks into the reduction. Keep whisking until they've tripled in volume and hold their weight; you'll see ribbon trails on top of the eggs.

2 Take the bowl off the heat and slowly pour in the butter a little at a time, as for mayonnaise, whisking all the time. The hollandaise must stay quite thick. Season with a balance of salt and lemon juice and keep warm, ready to serve.

NORTH-EAST

Hull and Grimsby were the centre of Britain's deep-sea fishing fleet until the 1970s, and you still get a sense of their former might. One legacy of deep-sea trawling is the number of quality fish-and-chip shops, which serve many different species of fish and also shellfish. Nowadays, the region also has smaller vessels landing local fish in places such as Eyemouth and Whitby, including some that are line-caught. Catfish (or wolf-fish) is a regional

'FOLLOW YOUR NOSE LIKE A CAT TO FIND TARRY SMOKEHOUSES WITH THEIR LACQUERED FISH.'

speciality better known by fishermen than landlubbers, and there are beautiful turbot and halibut too. Other species, such as squid and even red mullet, are starting to appear further north than before. Both locally and nationally, look out for North-East kippers, such as those from the Northumbrian villages of Craster and Seahouses and from Whitby in Yorkshire, where you can follow your nose like a cat to find the tarry smokehouses with their lacquered fish.

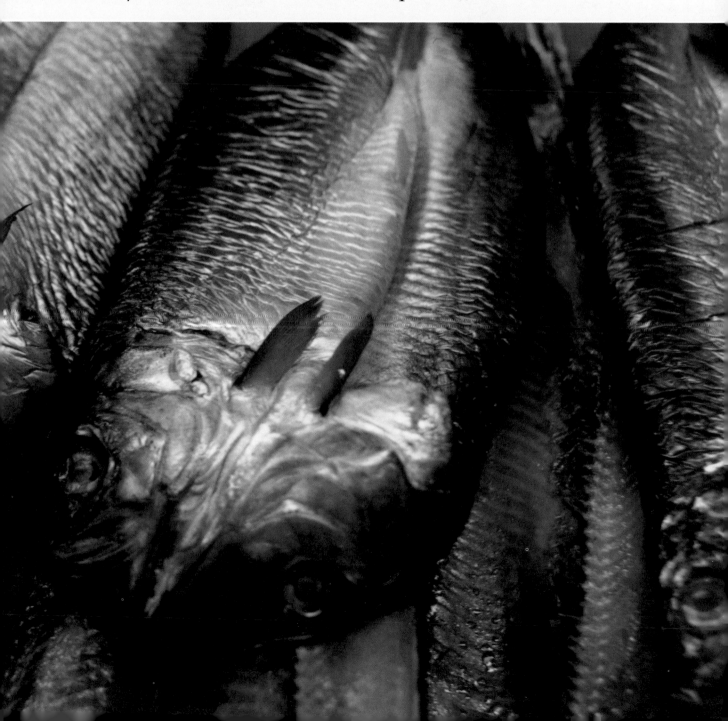

MUSTARD-ROAST TURBOT STEAKS, CRUSHED POTATOES AND SMOKED SALMON SAUCE

BRIAN TURNER CBE, CHEF-PATRON, BRIAN TURNER MAYFAIR, LONDON

Turbot is one of the finest fish caught in the North Sea, and this recipe marries its meaty texture with strong flavours.

serves 4

4 x 150g turbot steaks
1 tsp mustard powder
1 tsp flour
1 tbsp olive oil
75g unsalted butter
salt and pepper
2 shallots, peeled and finely chopped
1 tbsp white wine vinegar
125ml dry white wine
1 small bouquet garni (parsley, thyme, ½ bay leaf)
1 clove of garlic, peeled and crushed
150ml fish stock
150ml chicken stock
150ml double cream
100g smoked salmon, finely chopped
2 tomatoes, skinned, deseeded and roughly chopped
2 tbsp chopped fresh parsley
350g new potatoes
2 tbsp crème fraîche
1 tbsp finely chopped chives

1 Preheat the oven to 200°C/400°F/gas mark 6. Mix together the mustard and flour. Trim the turbot and dip the bone side into the mustard mixture.

2 Heat the oil with 50g butter. Dip the fish into the hot fat, mustard-side down. Season with salt and pepper. Colour and turn over, but do not colour the second side. Roast in the oven for 10 minutes, depending on the thickness of the fish, until cooked through.

3 Meanwhile, sweat the shallot in 25g butter, but do not colour. Add the white wine vinegar, white wine, bouquet garni and garlic, and reduce to a syrup.

4 Add the fish and chicken stocks and reduce by half. Add the double cream and reduce by half again.

5 Take the pan off the heat, add the smoked salmon, tomato and parsley, and season with salt and pepper.

6 Scrub the potatoes, then cook them in salted water, drain and dry. Crush the potatoes with a fork, add the crème fraîche and chives, and season.

7 Make a bed of potatoes in a ring and put the fish on top. Serve some sauce over and around the fish.

HALIBUT FILLET WITH A WILD MUSHROOM TOPPING

BRIAN TURNER CBE, CHEF-PATRON, BRIAN TURNER MAYFAIR, LONDON

'I prefer a mixture of fish stock and chicken stock, as this makes the sauce not too fishy, but if you are a non-meat eater then use just fish stock,' writes Brian Turner.

serves 4

4 x 175g halibut fillets
200g unsalted butter, plus extra for greasing
4 tbsp chopped fresh herbs (chives, chervil and parsley)
225g breadcrumbs
salt and pepper

100g wild mushrooms, finely chopped
2 hardboiled eggs
1 small glass dry white wine
300ml fish stock
300ml chicken stock
2 bay leaves
1 sprig of thyme
2 cloves of garlic, peeled
150ml double cream

1 Wash and pat dry the halibut fillets.

2 Beat 100g butter in bowl until soft and smooth. Add 2 tbsp chopped herbs and all the breadcrumbs, season and then slowly add the finely chopped mushrooms.

3 Pass the hardboiled eggs through a sieve and add to the mixture. Season with salt and pepper. Smear the mixture evenly on the bone side of the fish, cover and leave in a cool place to set for 20 minutes.

4 Preheat the oven to 200°C/400°F/gas mark 6. Lightly grease an ovenproof dish and lay the fillets crust-side upwards. Pour the wine, fish stock and chicken stock around the fish. Cut the bay leaves into thin strips using scissors and add to the liquor. Strip the leaves from the thyme and add to the liquid. Cut the garlic into thin strips and add to the dish.

5 Bake the fish in the oven until it is just cooked – around 10 minutes. Take the fillets out and carefully put them on to a greased baking sheet.

6 Strain and reduce the cooking liquor. Add the cream and continue to reduce. Add the remaining 100g butter, cut into cubes, and whisk in. Check the seasoning, then add the remaining 2 tbsp chopped herbs.

7 Meanwhile, place the fish under a hot grill to colour the topping. Serve surrounded by the sauce.

TOWER OF SCALLOPS AND SMOKED HADDOCK IN A PARSLEY SAUCE

BRIAN TURNER CBE, CHEF-PATRON, BRIAN TURNER MAYFAIR, LONDON

Haddock, one of the classic fish landed in the North-East, is also a fisherman's favourite. Here is it smoked and combined with elegant scallops and traditional parsley sauce.

serves 4

16 scallops, prepared, without roe
225g smoked haddock, skinned and boned
100g unsalted butter
3 shallots, peeled and chopped
1 clove of garlic, peeled and crushed
4 tomatoes, skinned, deseeded and roughly chopped
salt and pepper
125ml dry white wine
300ml fish stock
150ml double cream
2 tbsp chopped fresh parsley

1 Cut the scallops in half, crossways. Slice the haddock into pieces the same thickness as the scallops.

2 Melt 75g butter and sweat 2 of the chopped shallot, but do not colour. Add the garlic, then the tomato, then season with salt and pepper. Cook, stirring frequently, for 2 minutes, then take off the heat and cool.

3 In another pan, melt the remaining 25g butter, add another chopped shallot, and sweat but do not colour. Add the white wine and reduce by a quarter. Add the fish stock and double cream, and reduce by a quarter. Season with salt and pepper.

4 Meanwhile, layer the haddock and scallops in 5cm rings, putting the chopped tomatoes in the centre. Season with salt and pepper and steam for 6–8 minutes. Take out of the steamer, drain and put into a serving dish.

5 Add the parsley to the sauce and pour the sauce over the scallops and smoked haddock.

SHALLOW-FRIED POSH FISH FINGERS WITH PEA, LETTUCE AND MINT VINAIGRETTE

ANDREW PERN, CHEF-PATRON, THE STAR INN, HAROME, NORTH YORKSHIRE

Andrew Pern, born-and-bred in Yorkshire, is a gastropub chef who champions local produce. He gets his fish landed along the North-East coast — mostly at Scarborough, Whitby and North Shields — from Alan Hodgson, a fish merchant in Hartlepool. As well as using the fish in his cooking, Andrew sells it from the deli at The Star Inn, both fresh and prepared, and cooked into dishes such as smoked haddock cassoulet. 'People bring along their pots and we fill them up,' he says. Now that's what you'd call a real-food ready-meal. In this recipe he uses hot smoked salmon, from Yoadwath Mill, which is an excellent and convenient way to eat fish.

serves 4

2 shallots, peeled and finely chopped
1 tbsp unsalted butter
350g dry mashed potato (nothing added)
450g hot-smoked salmon, skinned and flaked
1 tbsp chopped garden herbs (parsley, chives and chervil), plus extra to garnish
½ tsp unwaxed lemon zest
juice of 1 lemon
salt and freshly ground black pepper

2 tbsp plain flour
2 eggs, beaten
100g breadcrumbs, flavoured with a pinch of fennel seeds
olive oil, for shallow-frying
a little plum tomato salad, to serve (optional)

for the green salad
2 tsp white wine vinegar
½ tsp English mustard
4 tsp olive oil
2 tsp chopped mint
100g fresh peas, cooked
75g cos, little gem or iceberg lettuce, finely shredded

1 Lightly sweat the shallot with the butter, without colouring, then add to the mash, flaked hot-smoked salmon, herbs, lemon zest and juice, and season if required. Let the mixture cool, then cover and chill in the refrigerator.

2 Preheat the oven to 180°C/350°F/gas mark 4. Put the flour, beaten eggs and breadcrumbs to coat the 'fingers' in three separate bowls.

3 Mould the smoked salmon mixture into approximately 6cm x 2cm x 2cm lengths. Pass the fish fingers first through the flour, then the egg, then the breadcrumbs. Repeat the egg and breadcrumb coatings for a second time to ensure a good coating. Keep in the refrigerator until ready to cook.

4 Shallow-fry the fish fingers until golden brown and finish in the oven until hot through. This takes just a few minutes.

5 To make the dressing, mix together the vinegar and English mustard, add the oil, then the mint and peas. Toss dressing with the lettuce.

6 Serve four fingers per main course portion, stacking two one way, then two on top the other way. Serve with the green salad and garnish with some chopped garden herbs. Place the tomato salad at the back of the plate, if using, and serve immediately.

DEEP-SEA TRAWLING

In the 19th century, industrialised deep-sea trawling made the fishing ports of Hull and Grimsby the biggest the world has ever seen. They were the centre of the distant-water fishing fleet that ventured to the icy waters of the far north in search of fish.

The origins of this fishing boom lie in 1843, when men from Brixham sailed to the North-East coast of England to find new fishing grounds. One boat made such an outstanding catch 60 miles from the Humber that it returned to land with its sides covered in fish scales; the place known as the Silver Pit had been discovered. It was part of the Dogger Bank, which became a watery mine of profits for Hull and Grimsby.

The 1840s railway boom meant the boats had access to bigger markets. When steam power was harnessed at sea, new fishing grounds could be reached in distant waters and the fish ferried back to shore more quickly. All this made fish a cheap alternative to meat for people living in Britain's burgeoning towns and cities.

But there was a human cost to this industrialized trawling. The system of apprenticeship meant workhouse children were forced to stay at sea, performing dangerous tasks under brutal conditions. The most dreaded job, carried out even on the roughest of seas in the flimsiest of crafts, was rowing the catch from the hauling boats to the ferrying ones.

The Royal National Mission to Deep Sea Fishermen (now commonly known as the Fishermen's Mission) was started by a Christian missionary, Ebenezer Mather, who went to sea to witness for himself the appalling conditions on these trawlers. He helped set up hospital ships so that crew members who had suffered injuries, such as lost limbs, could be treated immediately instead of having to wait until a boat went back to land.

British trawling increased in power and numbers until, by the 1950s, Hull and Grimsby had built up great fleets of mid- and distant-water trawlers. At the height, up to 17 per cent of Grimsby's population worked in fishing. This reliance on such a dangerous trade meant both places

could be devastated by tragedy. In 1954, Grimsby lost five ships at sea and 55 men. In 1968, 57 Hull men were lost in just a few weeks. Hull, overall, has lost more than 900 fishing boats to deep-sea fishing.

Life on a distant-water trawler was especially tough. A trip might take three weeks, with five days 'steaming out' – the phrase continues even in the days of diesel – to make the 2,000-mile round trip to Iceland, for example. Then there would be 18-hour days of continuous fishing. Whenever a haul comes in, there is a great buzz of adrenalin as everyone waits to see what they've got. There is no better feeling than when the catch is good. But a bad haul is a waste of time, worse still if the nets are damaged.

The constant hardship of this life at sea is not just the lack of sleep, but also the cold. A fisherman's hands and body go numb and nothing keeps out the cold, damp and wet. In the darkness his ears become his eyes, listening out, in particular, for the thunderous roar of waves. Every so often a big one comes and knocks everyone sideways, and you might go overboard if you haven't sensed its approach, bracing yourself in the brief second of quiet before it strikes.

For trawlermen, one of the satisfactions of the job is the feeling of being in a crew that works well together: a shipshape unit of men who rely on each other for their safety and livelihood. Fishing takes you to the fundamentals of existence; you are out in the elements with just your boat and your fellow men to keep you alive. At The National Fishing Heritage Centre in Grimsby you can, without an icy deck to contend with, get some idea of life on a distant-water trawler going out to the Arctic waters in the 1950s, and of what it was like for the family ashore, waiting for the safe return of the men.

The boom days of distant-water trawling ended when, along with the rising price of oil, countries began to defend the right to protect fishing off their shores. After the 'Cod War' of the 1970s, British fishing in Icelandic waters, pioneered by the trawlers of North-East England, was over.

LEFT TO RIGHT A trawler embarking on a routine 10-day fishing trip; a crew member at work; the skipper in the wheelhouse, from where he controls the nets while keeping a watchful eye on heavy machinery being operated below; Johnny 'Mince' Mackay finds his hat one of the safest places to keep his mending knife. BELOW Colin French and James Addison mending nets in between hauls.

SALAD OF RED MULLET, SAUCE GAZPACHO

MARCO PIERRE WHITE, FISHERMAN, CHEF AND RESTAURATEUR

This recipe, from Marco Pierre White's first book, White Heat, includes an exceptionally fresh and simple tomato sauce that goes well with any fish. It used to be that a red mullet swimming up the North-East coast of England had somewhat lost its way from the Mediterranean. But nowadays, with global warming, there are more found in the North Sea in the summertime, and they are increasingly common off the south of England.

serves 4

4 red mullet, filleted, skin-on
plain flour
olive oil, for frying

for the gazpacho sauce
500g cherry tomatoes
2 tsp white wine vinegar
1 tsp salt
1 tsp caster sugar
½ tsp freshly ground white
  pepper
100ml olive oil

*for the brunoise of ratatouille
  and salad*
olive oil, for frying
4 tsp each of very finely diced
  peeled courgette, fennel,
  yellow pepper and aubergine
16 leaves each of lamb's
  lettuce, frisée and oak leaf
60ml vinaigrette

1 To make the gazpacho sauce, in a blender or food processor, liquidize the tomatoes (including skin) with the vinegar. Add the salt, sugar and pepper and blend for 30 seconds. Keeping the machine running, add the olive oil slowly to incorporate. Pass the sauce through a muslin-lined sieve. Taste and adjust the seasoning.

2 For each fish, cut the fillets into squares of roughly 2.5cm, keeping the skin intact. Season with salt and pepper, and toss lightly in flour. Heat the olive oil in a frying pan over a high heat and fry the fish for around 30 seconds on each side. Drain on kitchen paper and keep warm. Warm four plates.

3 Put a little oil in a frying pan over a high heat and cook the finely chopped vegetables in it briefly until just cooked. Season.

4 Dress the lettuce with the vinaigrette.

5 Spoon the sauce in a circle around the edge of each warmed plate. Put the fish on the sauce, skin-side up and put five little piles of the ratatouille between the fish. Put a heap of the dressed salad in the centre.

FISH VELOUTÉ

MARCO PIERRE WHITE, FISHERMAN, CHEF AND RESTAURATEUR

Marco Pierre White's cooking, as well as being based on classic French preparations, such as this sauce for fish dishes, is founded on a thorough knowledge of raw ingredients. In the case of fish, this started as a boy when he went sea fishing from Bridlington, winning the Juvenile Trophy of the Bridlington Sea Fishing Festival two years running (and just missing out on a third triumphant year by a mere 225g). The trophy was an oak shield engraved with Flamborough Head, gently eroded by all the polishing of its proud young winners. When the competition fish had been landed, weighed and judged, they would often be given to the old folk, waiting on the quayside with their carrier bags for their supper.

makes about 1.1 litres

10 shallots, peeled and finely chopped
25g unsalted butter
750ml Noilly Prat
750ml fish stock
750ml double cream

1 Sweat the shallot in the butter over a moderate heat until soft but not coloured. Add the Noilly Prat and continue to cook until the mixture is syrupy – there should be almost no liquid left.

2 Add the fish stock and reduce by half over a high heat. Add the cream and bring the mixture back to the boil. Remove from the heat and leave in a warm place to infuse for 10 minutes.

3 Sieve the mixture. Keep any sauce you do not need in a covered bowl in the refrigerator for up to 2 days, or freeze.

CATFISH IN WHITE SAUCE

JOHN GILLIE, FORMER FISHERMAN, EYEMOUTH, NORTHUMBRIA

John Gillie was a skipper on a trawler, who fished out of Eyemouth for 20 years before, as he put it, his arm went AWOL in an accident in the harbour. He is grateful to the Fishermen's Mission for their subsequent help and was glad to send a recipe when he read about Best of British Fish in Fishing News. Catfish (or wolf-fish) is a catch fishermen like to take home for their own dinner. A white fish with a fearsome set of gnashers, its diet of shellfish gives it a good meaty texture. 'Strangely enough the ordinary public don't go for it,' says John. 'But fishermen are a bit more fussy and will go for less common fish when they taste good.'

serves 4 'easily'

- 1 whole catfish (about 2.25kg – ask your fishmonger to gut, skin and bone it)
- 1 onion, peeled and finely chopped
- vegetable or olive oil, for frying
- 2 carrots, finely chopped
- 4 button mushrooms, finely chopped
- 1 red pepper, deseeded and finely chopped
- 565ml vegetable stock, fresh or made with a cube
- 400g tinned chopped tomatoes
- juice of ½ lemon
- freshly ground black pepper
- 290ml full-fat milk
- 1 large knob of butter (about 20g)
- 2 tbsp plain white flour (about 20g)

1 Preheat the oven to 180°C/ 350°F/gas mark 4. Cut the fish into large chunks, 7.5–10cm across.

2 Gently fry the onion until soft in a little oil. Add the carrot and cook gently for another 5 minutes. Add the mushroom and cook for another 2 minutes. Add the red pepper and cook for another couple of minutes.

3 Add the fish to the vegetables, then add the stock, tomato and lemon juice. Season with salt and pepper.

4 Put the fish, vegetables and sauce in a casserole, cover and bake in the oven for 45 minutes.

5 Heat the milk just up to boiling point in a pan. Meanwhile, in another pan melt the butter and stir in the flour. Cook over a low heat for a couple of minutes, stirring, and then whisk or stir in the warmed milk; pour it in gradually at first so it mixes into the flour and butter, and then add the rest more quickly. Heat, stirring, until the sauce thickens. Season with salt and pepper to taste.

6 Serve the fish and vegetables dressed with the white sauce, with mashed potatoes or boiled basmati rice.

NORTH-WEST

The coast of North-West England includes the 122 square miles of Morecambe Bay, where cockles and brown shrimps have been harvested in commercial quantities ever since the railways brought large numbers of tourists in the 19th century. The fishermen need to know what they are doing out here. 'It's not like walking down a road, where you can take your bearings,' said one cockle picker. Mists can descend and disorientate as the tide rolls in

'THE TOP EN[D] THE CATCH W[ILL] COME HERE T[O] BE SOLD FOR TH[E] FISHMONGERS' SLABS.'

suddenly over the sands. Cockles are also picked further down on the River Dee estuary, and the shrimps caught off Southport are potted in butter and spices, as are the Morecambe Bay ones. Fleetwood's wholesale fish market is now targeted at prime produce: the top end of the trawlers' catch will come here to be sold for the fishmongers' slabs. The food lovers of the area enjoy local wild sea bass, skate, mackerel, monkfish, halibut and plaice in particular.

SZECHUAN SALT-AND-PEPPER BABY SQUID

MARK PRESCOTT, CHEF-PATRON, THE MULBERRY TREE, WRIGHTINGTON, LANCASHIRE

In the 16 years Mark Prescott spent working for the Roux Brothers, latterly as head chef at Le Gavroche, he learnt about the primary importance of good raw ingredients, not least when cooking fish. He and his business partner James Moore get great fish from their supplier Chris Neve, who has his own trawlers and buys on Fleetwood Market. Some of Mark's favourites from the local catch include thick, meaty skate wings, wild sea bass, line-caught if possible, and the large plaice that can be 5cm thick in their prime. The Mulberry Tree is at the forefront of the gastropub revolution in Britain, which is getting more people to enjoy different types of fish. When the pair took over the pub in 2000, most of the orders would be for steaks; now around 60 per cent of the starters and main courses offered are based on seafood.

serves 4

320g baby squid (more tender than larger squid, but you could use that too)
1 clove of garlic, peeled (optional)
2 tsp unroasted sesame oil
2 medium red chillies, to taste, finely chopped
2 standard green chillies, to taste, finely chopped
4 spring onions, finely chopped

for the dipping sauce
300g caster sugar
150ml lemon vinegar (or use more white wine vinegar)
150ml white wine vinegar
2 medium red chillies, to taste, finely chopped

2 medium green chillies, to taste, finely chopped
4 spring onions, finely chopped

for the salt-and-pepper seasoning
100g Maldon sea salt
15g cracked black peppercorns
10g ground coriander
5g ground pink peppercorns
10g ground Szechuan peppercorns
pinch of ground ginger
pinch of celery salt

for the garnish (optional)
4 rectangles banana leaf (can't be eaten)
lime wedges
sprigs of fresh coriander

1 To make the dipping sauce, boil the sugar and vinegars together until they have reduced to a thick syrup. Allow to cool for 20 minutes. Add the chillies and spring onion to the cooled syrup.

2 Make the salt-and-pepper seasoning by mixing together all the ingredients.

3 To prepare the squid, take everything out of the body sac. Cut off the beak and remove the quill (if you are using a large squid you will have to remove the ink sac and take the membrane off the body, but the baby squid require less preparation). Keep the tentacles whole. Wash the tentacles and body thoroughly and dry. Slice the prepared and cleaned squid as finely as possible. Season to taste with the salt-and-pepper mix, depending on how spicy you want the dish to be; a generous teaspoon is enough for this quantity – the rest will keep well in an airtight container.

4 Chop the clove of garlic as finely as possible, if using. Put the sesame oil in a preheated, thick-bottomed sauté pan. The pan has to be really hot or the squid will boil rather than fry. When the oil starts to smoke, add the squid. Toss it quickly in the oil, adding the chillies, spring onion and garlic. The cooking time should be no more than 90 seconds. Serve immediately with the dipping sauce and garnishes.

BAKED LOIN OF COD WITH A LANCASHIRE CHEESE AND BASIL CRUST AND VERMOUTH AND CHIVE CREAM

MARK PRESCOTT, CHEF-PATRON, THE MULBERRY TREE, WRIGHTINGTON, LANCASHIRE

This complex, sophisticated dish makes full use of the chef's system of advance preparation, or mis en place, and such planning can fit well into a home dinner party; you do most of the work before your guests arrive, putting the fish in the oven at the last minute so it cooks as you eat your starter. When Mark makes this dish at his restaurant, he uses cod landed in Fleetwood that has been caught in the Irish Sea.

serves 4

4 x 225g prime cod loin steaks
  (thick head of the fillet only)
about 2 tsp Dijon mustard
fish stock or white wine, or a
  mixture, to cook
1 tbsp finely chopped chives

for the basil crust
80g fresh white breadcrumbs
30g fresh basil
40g Lancashire cheese, finely
  grated
20g mozzarella, finely grated
40g butter

for the mushroom duxelles
1 large shallot, peeled and
  finely chopped
a little butter
200g small button mushrooms,
  very finely chopped
50ml double cream

for the tomato fondue
1 large shallot, peeled and
  finely chopped
1 clove of garlic, peeled and
  finely chopped
50ml olive oil
8–10 ripe plum tomatoes,
  skinned, deseeded and
  chopped
1 tbsp tomato purée
1 bay leaf
salt and pepper

for the vermouth cream
2 large shallots, peeled and
  finely chopped
a little butter
1 sprig of lemon thyme
200ml Noilly Prat
200ml fish stock (optional)
400ml double cream

1 To make the crust, place the breadcrumbs and basil in a food processor and blend until bright green. Add the remaining ingredients and blend until smooth. Spread on to a foil-covered baking tray in a layer 2mm thick and freeze.

2 Once frozen, cut into four 8cm x 5cm rectangles. Peel off the foil.

3 To make the mushroom duxelles, sweat the shallot in the butter until softened but not coloured, then add the mushroom and cook over a very low heat until cooked through and as dry as possible. Add the cream to bind.

4 To make the tomato fondue, sweat the shallot and garlic in the olive oil until transparent. Add the tomato, tomato purée and bay leaf. Cook over a low heat until almost dry, stirring often. Season and remove the bay leaf.

5 To make the vermouth cream, sweat the shallot in butter without colouring. Add the lemon thyme, Noilly Prat and fish stock, if using. Boil over a high heat to reduce by half. Add the cream, bring to the boil and then turn off the heat.

6 Preheat the oven to 200°C/400°F/gas mark 6.

7 Smear each loin with ½ tsp Dijon mustard, or to taste, then spread with equal layers, about 2mm thick, of the tomato fondue and mushroom duxelles. Top with a basil crust rectangle. Place in a heavy casserole dish and pour in the fish stock or white wine, or a mixture, until the liquid comes a third of the way up the fish. Cook in the oven for 6–7 minutes. If there is any liquid left, you can add it to the vermouth cream.

8 Boil the vermouth cream, blend and finish with freshly chopped chives. Serve immediately with the fish. New potatoes, baby vegetables and spinach go well with this.

WHOLE SALT-BAKED, GILT-HEADED BREAM WITH A CHORIZO AND MORECAMBE BAY SHRIMP RISOTTO

MARK PRESCOTT, CHEF-PATRON, THE MULBERRY TREE, WRIGHTINGTON, LANCASHIRE

Mark recommends the Mediterranean gilt-headed bream as a good-value fish which looks like a substantial meal if you serve it on the bone. (For a more local fish, he uses skinned skate wings.) Here he has partnered it with a risotto flavoured with brown shrimps, which he gets from Morecambe Bay.

serves 4

4 x 680g gilt-head bream, scaled and gutted
coarse sea salt
olive oil
juice of 1 lemon

for the garnish
4 lemon segments
20g long Parmesan shavings
chervil sprigs

for the risotto
1 generous knob of butter (about 30g)
1 large shallot, peeled and finely chopped
1 small onion, peeled and finely chopped
200g arborio rice
1 fresh bay leaf
100ml dry white wine
600ml shellfish stock (or vegetable or chicken stock)
60g chorizo sausage, finely diced
60g peeled, cooked brown shrimps
50g fresh parsley, chopped
100g Parmesan, finely grated
100g mascarpone cheese

1 To cook the risotto, put the butter in a saucepan and sweat the shallot and onion over a low heat until transparent. Turn up the heat and add the rice and bay leaf. Cook over a high heat, stirring, for 2 minutes and add the wine. Turn down the heat. Stir until the wine is absorbed. Add a third of the stock. Allow the rice to absorb the stock, this time stirring only when adding the stock so you do not break up the grains. Repeat. Continue to cook gradually, adding the last third of the stock a bit at a time, until the rice is plump and creamy. This will take about 18 minutes. Add the chorizo, shrimps, parsley, grated Parmesan and mascarpone. Beat until smooth and creamy. Season to taste and serve immediately with the bream.

2 To cook the bream, preheat the oven to 220°C/425°F/gas mark 7. On a griddle or thick-bottomed, cast-iron pan, add a good handful of coarse sea salt and heat. When the salt starts to jump, add a splash of olive oil. Add the bream and colour for 3–4 minutes. Turn over and place in the oven for 7–8 minutes.

3 Remove from the oven and squeeze a very fresh lemon over the fish. Place the fish carefully on top of the risotto and garnish with lemon wedges, Parmesan shavings and sprigs of chervil.

GRAVADLAX

STEVEN DOHERTY, CHEF, FIRST FLOOR CAFÉ, LAKELAND LIMITED, WINDERMERE, CUMBRIA

'It is fine to use farmed salmon for this simple Scandinavian-inspired starter,' writes chef Steven Doherty. 'Besides, what a waste it would be to use beautiful wild salmon. I know there are issues about farmed salmon, but it has a place in the market. Like everything it simply needs to be handled carefully and controlled intelligently.'

serves 10

50g white peppercorns
50g dried dill weed
50g caster sugar

1kg coarse sea salt
1 fully trimmed, unskinned
   side of salmon, boned
   (approx. 2kg)
25g Dijon mustard

1 Coarsely grind the peppercorns, then mix together with 25g dill, the sugar and salt.

2 Put the salmon in a deep tray and cover both sides with the salt mixture. Cover and leave in a cold place for 24 hours.

3 Remove the salmon from the salt mixture and rinse under cold running water. Dry the salmon on a wire tray in a cold place for 48 hours.

4 On a piece of greaseproof paper, coat both sides of the salmon with Dijon mustard and the remainder of the dried dill. Shake off the excess dill and keep it to use another time. Cure in a cold place for 24 hours.

5 Slice thinly or wrap in cling film and refrigerate. The salmon will keep well for 2 weeks. Serve with the sweet grain mustard dressing.

*for the sweet grain mustard
   dressing*

100g Dijon mustard
100g grain mustard
65g caster sugar

a splash white wine vinegar, to
   taste
a dribble of sunflower oil, or
   until you get the right
   consistency
10g dried dill weed

1 Mix all the ingredients together. This will keep for 1 month in an airtight container in the refrigerator.

POTTED SHRIMPS

GILES SHAW, FISHMONGER, WELLGATE FISHERIES, CLITHEROE, LANCASHIRE

Giles Shaw pots brown shrimps for his fishmonger's shop and here gives his tip for making sure the shrimps aren't too swamped in butter. This is a favourite British regional dish and the very best form of convenience food. Try potted shrimps stirred into scrambled eggs, or pasta, or simply warmed through and served on toast.

makes 8 ramekins

225g butter
pinch of mace or nutmeg, to taste
pinch of cayenne, to taste
450g brown shrimps

1 Melt the butter in a pan. Add the spices, to taste. Add the shrimps and bring to just below boiling point. Turn down the heat and cook on a low heat for 2–3 minutes.

2 Drain off the butter and reserve. Put the shrimps into eight pots or ramekins, cool and then chill in the refrigerator.

3 Take out of the refrigerator and press the shrimps down slightly with another pot (this stops you needing to use so much butter). Reheat the reserved butter and pour over just to cover the shrimps and chill again until the butter sets.

FISH AND CHIPS

Seniors chippie, on the outskirts of Blackpool, serves up showtime as well as sustenance. On one side of a bank of fryers rustling with crisping batter is the take-away queue, kept entertained by a plasma screen flashing up images of champion halibut and newsreel of the 1970s cod wars. On the other side is the restaurant, painted Mediterranean turquoise and sandy yellow, with an artwork aquarium full fishy facts. There's Moët on the menu as well as mushy peas.

Some regulars come to Seniors as often as four times a week. Two dozen come three times and about 50 couples come twice a week, often for the set meal of cod and small chips and a drink for £5.50. Both locals and occasionals tuck into great platefuls and record their appreciation in the visitors' book. A customer from France writes that Seniors is 'génial'; the trade unionist Brenda Dean says she'll be back; Russ Abbott came regularly when he was doing panto. One admirer has left a lipstick kiss; another quips, 'The catfish and chips left us both purring.'

Cleanliness is next to codliness at Seniors. The need for the highest standards was one of the aims of the owners, Rick and Janet Horabin, when they bought the place as a semi-retirement job after Rick had spent nearly 30 years selling fish to the trade. He and his son Alastair buy daily on Fleetwood market and keep the stock flowing fast. As a result of energetic attention to detail, the place has a pristine pizzazz.

Another part of Rick's mission is to take the wide variety of British fish to the masses. To start with, the 'Magnificent Seven' went on the menu: cod, haddock, plaice, scampi, hake, lemon sole and John Dory. Now it is the 'Magnificant 12', with the addition of halibut, skate, turbot, brill and Torbay soles. There are also exotics, such as catfish. John Dory is the restaurant's signature fish, displayed on the staff shirts and on Rick's van, with its registration plate of DI ORY. The meaty fillets from this firm fish are rarely found in chip shops, let alone at such competitive prices.

Brendan Smith has fried the fish here for 23 years. He stands at the bubbling sizzle of the fryers like a skipper on the bridge. How does he tell the difference between all the different types of fish in the fryer? The fillets are cut into slightly different shapes to help.

Jeannie Wadeson, Seniors most long-standing waitress, has nurtured the customers for 19 years with her warm welcome and big smile. When trying a new fish, she and her staff act as ambassadors for the unusual, giving out tasters to tempt people to try an alternative to cod and haddock. Full of genuine enthusiasm for the red snapper and shark, she has slowly expanded the customers' choices.

At the most manic times, such as Friday nights, when hundreds pass through this family-sized business, the pace is fast but ordered and friendly. Rick rolls up his sleeves and helps out; his sons are there in the thick of the action.

The business is in the heart of the fishing community. Rick's sons and some of the staff did a charity run in aid of the Fishermen's Mission and the Mission's collecting box sits by the cash register along with the collection for the lifeboats. Rick is in the process of setting up a school to teach fish filleting to the long-term unemployed; there is a skills shortage in this part of the food chain.

It is uncertain who first put fish and chips together, but the combination soon gained a hold on the nation's taste in the industrialized North West in the 19th century. In the cotton towns of the Pennines, where wives and mothers worked, cooking space, time and budgets were tight and this great take-away thrived, providing tasty, filling food for generations. In nutritional terms, fish and chips compares favourably with fast-food pizzas and curries.

The growth of the chippie was a powerful factor behind the industrialization of fishing, from cottage industry to big trawlers and large ports. The trawlers went to distant fishing grounds to supply a trade that grew to at least 35,000 shops in the 1930s. Some districts of cities such as Leeds had a chippie in every street, often people opening up for business for a couple of hours in their front room.

Potato crisps took off because chip-shop owners wanted to keep fryers busy, and the fishing fleet, built up by the demands of chippies, played an important role in wartime by feeding people and forming part of the merchant navy.

TOP, LEFT TO RIGHT **Customers dining at Seniors chippie; serving the fish and chips; Rick Horabin, who opened Seniors after 30 years of selling fish to the trade.** BELOW, CLOCKWISE FROM LEFT **Jeannie Wadeson, who has been waitressing at Seniors for 19 years; John Dory at Fleetwood market; proprietors Rick and Janet Horabin; John Dory is the restaurant's signature fish.**

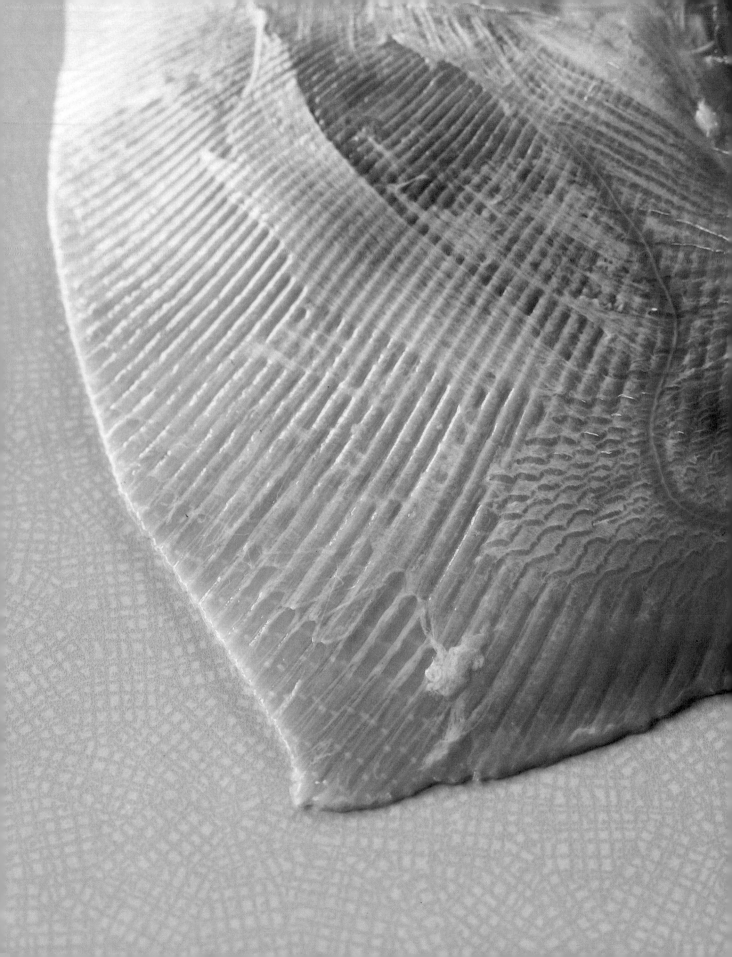

SKATE WINGS ON PAK CHOI WITH MELTING POTTED SHRIMPS

NIGEL HAWORTH, CHEF-PATRON, NORTHCOTE MANOR, LANGHO, LANCASHIRE

As a boy, Nigel Haworth fished for skate off the Welsh coast. It is one of his favourite fish, both to watch as it swims gracefully in the sea, and to cook and eat. In kitchen tests that he did for fish and chips, skate came out top for flavour. Here, he partners it with the fresh flavours of mint and pak choi, and the rich nuggets of locally potted shrimps.

serves 2

2 x 250g skate wings (ask your fishmonger to remove the cartilage)
20g chopped onion
40g unsalted butter
500ml light chicken stock
2 sprigs of mint
salt
100g pak choi
2 x 60g pots of potted shrimps
pinch of chopped fresh chives

1 Soften the chopped onion in 15g butter in a large heavy-bottomed pan. Add the chicken stock and mint and bring the stock up to the boil. Add a pinch of salt to taste.

2 Put the skate wings in the stock and cover with a lid. Simmer for 2 minutes, then remove the pan from the heat.

3 Warm a sauté pan and add the remaining 25g butter. Add the pak choi, a pinch of salt and a little of the stock. Sauté briefly until the pak choi is lightly cooked – just to soften. Place the pak choi in the centre of two serving bowls.

4 Place the skate on top of the pak choi, put the potted shrimps on top and place under a hot grill until the potted shrimps start to melt. Sprinkle with chives and serve.

WEST SCOTLAND & THE WESTERN ISLES

On the westerly fringe of Scotland, fishing traditionally provided a crucial part of the crofters' diet, and the habit remains of catching a few mackerel or getting some shellfish for supper. Some of the most delicious seafood in Britain comes from these clean coastal waters, and it ends up in high-quality restaurants and fishmongers, not just here, but also abroad. Best of all, though, is to eat it locally. There is a mobile van in Tobermory, on Mull, that even sells scallops and chips. The chefs in this region revel in the quality of their raw ingredients, and to sit at their tables and enjoy the sweet, ozone freshness of this catch is to experience regional produce at its finest and freshest. But the fishermen can take risks to get it. The west coast and its islands can be lashed with rough weather, and the Mission's office in Stornoway, on Lewis, is one of its busiest.

'TO ... ENJOY THE SWEET OZONE-FRESHNESS OF THIS CATCH IS TO EXPERIENCE REGIONAL PRODUCE AT ITS FINEST.'

SMOKED HADDOCK CREAMY STEW WITH SHALLOTS, SPINACH AND SAFFRON

CLAIRE MACDONALD, FOOD WRITER AND HOTELIER, KINLOCH LODGE, SLEAT, ISLE OF SKYE

'I am lucky enough to live in the south of Skye,' writes Claire Macdonald. 'Our shellfish, caught locally, is the envy of the world. There is none better — anywhere! Our local fish merchant, John Gilbertson, of Isle of Skye Seafoods, lives just seven miles from Kinloch, where we live and work — our home is a hotel. Over the 32 years we have been running the hotel the range of fish we buy and serve has varied. But what it has in common is its freshness. We never serve tuna, for instance, because it is not a locally caught fish. Our guests come to Skye to eat local fish and shellfish.

'This is a heavenly dish using smoked haddock. The art of preserving fish by smoking is truly a Scottish art. I don't think you need anything else to eat with it — possibly bread, or even plain boiled potatoes.'

serves 6

900g–1.25kg undyed
   smoked haddock fillets
8–10 shallots, peeled
3 tbsp extra-virgin olive oil

600ml double cream
2 good pinches of saffron
   strands
freshly ground black pepper
100g fresh baby leaf spinach

1 Feel the smoked haddock with your fingertips for bones and pull any out. Cut the filleted fish into chunks about 3cm wide.

2 Chop the shallot very finely. Heat the olive oil in a large sauté pan and sauté the shallot until it is quite soft but not coloured. Add the pieces of fish, cream and saffron and gently simmer. The fish will take about 3 minutes to cook, depending to a certain extent on the width of your sauté pan.

3 Season with plenty of pepper — no salt will be needed for most tastes because the smoked haddock should be sufficiently salty. Add the spinach. It will be a high mound, but cover the pan with a lid and the spinach will wilt very quickly.

4 When the spinach has wilted right down, carefully — so as not to break up the pieces of fish more than you can help — combine it evenly with the rest of the contents of the sauté pan. Ladle into warmed bowls to serve.

5 You can prepare your fish hours in advance or even the previous day. Keep it in a covered bowl in the refrigerator. Similarly, you can chop and sauté the shallots well in advance, so all you need to do before eating is to assemble the ingredients and cook them.

SEARED SCALLOPS WITH SPICY CAULIFLOWER PURÉE

CLAIRE MACDONALD, FOOD WRITER AND HOTELIER, KINLOCH LODGE, SLEAT, ISLE OF SKYE

The scallops growing in the clean Hebridean waters are famous for their high quality, and their sweet meatiness is set off beautifully by this simple recipe.

serves 6

18 king scallops (3 per person)
1 tbsp olive oil
2 shallots, peeled and chopped
2 cauliflowers, cut into florets
3 tbsp double cream
1 tsp dried chilli flakes
salt and freshly ground black pepper

1 Brush each scallop on both sides with a little olive oil.

2 Sauté the chopped shallot in the remaining olive oil until soft but not coloured. Steam the cauliflower. When it is cooked, mix with the cooked shallot, purée it and stir in the cream, chilli flakes, a good pinch of salt and a grinding of black pepper – this can be kept warm for up to 1 hour.

3 Just before serving, heat a large frying pan and add the scallops; they will need about 1 minute on each side. Serve the scallops on top of the cauliflower purée.

POTTED CRAB

CLAIRE MACDONALD, FOOD WRITER AND HOTELIER, KINLOCH LODGE, ISLE OF SKYE

'I was born and spent part of my growing-up years near Morecambe Bay, where the shrimps come from,' writes Claire Macdonald. 'These tiny, slightly peppery tasting crustacea are delicious potted: they are tossed in melted butter flavoured with mace, then packed in small pots and sealed with melted butter. But for potted crab, the melted butter to bind the crab meat is altogether too rich — crab is so very rich a shellfish. Instead I use a small amount of mayonnaise. It is, I hope you will agree, an utterly delicious way to eat crab.'

serves 6

675g equal quantities white and brown crab meat, mixed well
2 tbsp mayonnaise
6 sprigs of dill
175g butter, melted

for the mayonnaise
1 egg and 1 egg yolk
1 level tsp caster sugar
½ tsp salt
plenty of freshly ground black pepper
1 level tsp mustard powder
2 tsp Tabasco
300ml olive oil
juice of 1 lemon

1 Make the mayonnaise by putting the whole egg, yolk, sugar, salt, pepper, mustard powder and Tabasco into a processor and whizzing, gradually adding the olive oil. When you have a thick emulsion, add the lemon juice.

2 Mix the crab meat into 2 tbsp of the mayonnaise, and divide evenly between six ramekins. Smooth, and put a small sprig of dill on each. Carefully pour melted butter over the surface of each ramekin and put the ramekins into the refrigerator until you are ready to serve them.

3 Serve with Melba toast, which can be made a day in advance and kept in a sealed polythene bag.

INSHORE FISHING

Inshore fishermen patch together a living from different sources, netting and trawling for fish and putting out shellfish pots, or creels, as they are called in Scotland. Ian MacKinnon, on the West of Scotland, is one of a new breed of small-scale fishermen who have diversified yet further. He counterbalances the unpredictability of creel fishing in the heavy, jumping, open sea with a steadily growing income from his mussel farm in the beautiful 'Loch of Caves', Loch Nan Uamh, on the west coast of the Highlands.

Ian's rope-grown mussels are a high-quality, sustainable product, grown to plumpness in good waters and harvested when they are ready and needed. His 'office' has a backdrop of mountains falling down to clear, clean water. In the spring he puts 10-metre ropes into the loch so that microscopic mussel spat, floating in the water, can attach themselves, eventually mooring with what in the adult mussel is known as the 'beard'. By August the ropes have bloomed with a mass of tiny mussels, each the size of a pinhead. Ian can watch his crop progress: the water is so clear that he can see five or six metres down. The mussels feed by filtering the floating buffet of larvae, spat and other micro-organisms. The ropes are pegged at intervals so the shellfish don't slide down as they swell to maturity in about two years.

As Ian works, there is other marine life to contemplate: the starfish, anemones, crabs, huge spaceships of jellyfish and, occasionally, the otters that play on the rocks. This is a beautiful spot, just south of Skye, on this coastline of islands and inlets. Bonny Prince Charlie hid in one of the caves; the loch has grand horizons, with views of the Hebrides, yet it's also secluded from the rest of the world.

It took six years from applying for a mussel farming licence for Ian to get his first harvest. He has reinvested any money spare from his creel fishing, buying new ropes to expand this maritime field of shellfish. Now the source of his income varies between 60–80 per cent mussels and 20–40 per cent fishing. Every day, he gets a text message from his main seller, fishmonger Andy Race in Mallaig, and harvests the mussels that are needed, to order. Within hours they can be on a restaurant table, steamed open in a fragrant broth.

Ian started fishing to find a more fulfilling life than he had ashore. After studying agricultural economics and applied biology at Glasgow University, he went through a series of jobs, but his mind floated back to childhood holidays with his grandfather on the Hebridean island of Eigg, where going to sea to supplement your diet was a normal part of life. Ian had always thought he would eventually retire and go fishing. 'I'm glad I didn't wait that long,' he reflects now.

One day he went to a wedding and extracted a promise from a tipsy skipper that he'd take him to sea. There followed months of pestering before he got a berth. After an 18-month apprenticeship, he bought a boat, then another, spending £17,000 on the vessel and £20,000 on the gear 20 years ago (the cost, even on this small scale, would be double this now, plus the £5,000 for a fishing licence).

Life at sea is full of dangers and financial risk. While Ian has made as much as £764 in one day from creel fishing, he has also made £214 in three months because of poor weather and losing his gear. Seeing at least one fishing acquaintance die almost every year was part of his motivation for running the mussel farm. He is now in a position where he no longer feels he must go out in bad weather for his haul of velvet and brown crabs, prawns and lobsters. Ian estimates that full-time creel fishermen put their life on the line 100 days out of every 300.

For five years, Ian featured on the BBC TV series 'Video Nation', talking about what he did and why, and so is in a better position than most to explain his way of life. He describes the daily changing beauty of the sea, sky and land; coming back to shore in the winter as the setting sun paints the cliffs blood-red, with one part of the sky evening blue, the other black and starry. The weather can also be terrible for days and days.

But there is an underlying satisfaction to Ian's life that lasts longer than good weather — or bad: the satisfaction of feeling part of a tradition of West Highlander fishermen, leading an independent life in close contact with the world around them.

BELOW Ian MacKinnon, inshore day-boat fisherman and mussel farmer. ABOVE Ian rowing out to his inshore boat.

SCALLOP AND BASIL SALAD

ALISON OAKES, MARINE-DIVED SCALLOPS, ISLE OF SKYE

Alison Oakes' husband David dives for scallops in the waters around the Isle of Skye. He also collects the scallop spat and re-lays them on the seabed at Loch Sligachan, beside the beautiful Cuillin Mountains, harvesting the mature scallops after six or seven years. David and Alison have run their business Oakes' Marine Dived Scallops for 15 years, and now sell to local restaurants, including the celebrated Three Chimneys, and to a local processor who sends their shellfish around the country. This is the dish they most like to make with their own produce.

serves 4

50g sun-dried tomatoes in olive oil, drained
small bunch fresh basil
4 tbsp walnut or sesame oil
2 tbsp red wine vinegar
a selection of salad leaves
2 tbsp extra virgin olive oil
16 scallops (white meat only)

1 Roughly chop the sun-dried tomatoes and tear the basil.

2 Whisk together the walnut or sesame oil and red wine vinegar in a bowl. Stir in the tomatoes and basil.

3 Place the salad leaves on four small plates.

4 Heat the olive oil in a wok on a high heat and fry the scallops until well browned (about 3 minutes). Stir in the tomato and basil mixture, then pour it on to the cold salad and serve.

RAZOR SHELLS

IAN STEPHEN AND DONALD URQUHART, AUTHOR, MACKEREL & CREAMOLA

Ian Stephen is an artist, writer and former coastguard who lives on the Isle of Lewis. His book of stories, drawings and recipe-poems, Mackerel & Creamola, embraces children's drawings of billowing skate and tales of Hebridean voyages, as well as instructions on how you make tea on a boat. Ian describes recipes as 'a conversation'. Razor shells are a delicacy picked from sandy beaches at a low spring tide during cold months with an 'r' in their name. You can sometimes find them in fishmongers. At the end of the book are more recipes by the artist Donald Urquhart, and this is his one for razor shells. He calls it 'the hangover cure from heaven'.

serves 2

12 razor clams
salad leaves

130ml olive oil
a couple of pinches of freshly
    grated root ginger
2 tbsp balsamic vinegar

1 On a clean beach dig out 12 good–sized razor clams, or, after a storm, pick them up – but they must be fresh and alive. Place the razors in a bucket of sea water. Discard any razor clams that have cracked shells or shells that do not close when tapped.

2 Arrange the salad leaves on a plate. Heat the oil in a wok then add the razor shells. As soon as they begin to open, add the grated root ginger. Continue cooking for a minute or two, shaking the wok frequently.

3 When the shells are open (discard any that don't), lift them out of the wok and arrange on the salad leaves. Discard any clams that do not open. Return the wok to the heat and add the vinegar to the oil – immediately pour this hot dressing over the shells and then serve.

ANDY'S LOW-FAT CULLEN SKINK

ANDY RACE, FISH MERCHANT AND SMOKER, MALLAIG, HIGHLANDS

'I love traditional Cullen skink, but find it rather rich,' writes Andy Race. 'With healthy living in mind as well, I have played around with the ingredients to form this simple recipe which does nothing to compromise flavour. I usually make this up from anything tasty left on the fish counter and would encourage you to have fun and experiment yourself, using whatever you find that looks fresh, without sticking rigidly to a set recipe. The one thing you must include, though, is smoked white fish – undyed. For a treat, throw in a few bits of prawn, lobster or any other shellfish, such as razor clams, but it's better to avoid crab. Finally, aim to put in small amounts of different coloured ingredients so that the soup looks pretty – such as tiny amounts of red or yellow pepper, peas, etc.'

serves 4

1 rasher back bacon, chopped
1 medium onion, peeled and finely chopped
2 tsp olive oil
2 tsp plain flour
300ml semi-skimmed milk
2 medium potatoes, peeled and diced
1 medium celery stick, finely sliced
2 medium carrots, diced
450g undyed smoked haddock fillet, skinned
225g white fish fillet, skinned (e.g. coley, cod, haddock)
225g fresh salmon, boned and cubed
12 mussels, scrubbed and beards removed and/or 4 scallops
1 tbsp chopped smoked salmon trimmings

1 Slowly fry the bacon and onion in the olive oil until soft and pale – about 7–10 minutes.

2 Stir in the flour and cook for 2 minutes. Remove from the heat and gradually add the milk and 600ml water, stirring constantly. Cook, stirring, until the soup comes to the boil and thickens. Lower the heat.

3 Add the potato, celery and carrot (and any other vegetables you want to use). Cover and simmer very gently for 25–30 minutes, or until the vegetables are tender.

4 Cut the haddock and white fish into cubes. Discard any mussels that have cracked shells or shells that do not close when tapped. Add the fish and shellfish to the soup. Simmer for 5–7 minutes. Discard any mussels that have not opened. Season to taste with salt and pepper, and serve piping hot.

BRACADALE CRAB WITH NEW POTATO, CUCUMBER AND DILL SALSA

SHIRLEY SPEAR, CHEF-PATRON, THE THREE CHIMNEYS, COLBOST, ISLE OF SKYE

'The Three Chimneys is in a beautiful, remote corner of north-west Skye, on the shores of Loch Dunvegan, a wide sea loch that opens out to The Minch', writes Shirley Spear. 'I can see the prawn boats heading out to sea in the early morning from my bedroom window and watch them returning later in the day with precious cargo destined for my restaurant tables that evening. This is a delicious, very simple starter using fresh crab meat, new potatoes, cucumber and fresh herbs from local growers who supply me with a wealth of perfect ingredients to accompany the catch-of-the-day. Being able to serve seafood when it is so fresh and of such high quality is something I feel immensely proud to do as a Scottish chef. I have a good working relationship with a number of creel fishermen and scallop divers, as well as those who farm oysters and mussels.'

serves 6–8

for the crab topping
1 tbsp good-quality mayonnaise
1 tsp Dijon mustard
500g fresh mixed brown and white crab meat
juice of 1 lemon
salt and white pepper

for the salsa
about 24 baby new potatoes (a waxy, salad variety)
2 large cucumbers, peeled, halved and deseeded
8 spring onions, finely chopped
2 large green chillies, halved, deseeded and finely chopped
2 fat cloves of garlic, peeled and crushed
2 tbsp baby capers (drain the brine)
1 tbsp chopped fresh dill
2 tbsp chopped flat-leaf parsley
rind of 2 unwaxed limes, finely grated
juice of 4 limes
2 tbsp good-quality olive oil, plus extra to garnish
caster sugar (optional)
a few fresh herb sprigs (e.g. tarragon, flat-leaf parsley, dill, sorrel and salad burnet), to garnish

1 For the crab topping, mix the mayonnaise and mustard together. Add the crab meat, then the lemon juice. Season to taste. Cover and refrigerate.

2 For the salsa, wash the potatoes. Put them in a pan of cold salted water, bring to the boil and simmer until just beginning to go soft. Strain and set aside until cool enough to handle.

3 Meanwhile, prepare the salsa. Chop the cucumber into small pieces the same size as the capers. Mix the cucumber, spring onion and chilli together.

4 Add the garlic, capers, dill and parsley. Add the grated lime rind and half the lime juice (do not add all the juice at first, in case it is too much). Add 2 tbsp olive oil to help bind the ingredients. Mix, season with salt and pepper, and taste. You may need to add more lime juice or a large pinch of caster sugar.

5 While the potatoes are still warm, cut them into small dice. Place them in a clean bowl and gently stir in the salsa. Chill for up to 1 hour before serving, to allow the potatoes to soften and soak up the flavours.

6 To serve, place a ring mould in the centre of a serving plate and fill two-thirds of the way up with the salsa. Pack it in well. Top this with the crab meat – the crab will be a few centimetres higher than the top of the mould. Carefully remove the mould. Garnish with a few fresh herbs on top. Drizzle olive oil over the herbs and around the tian.

NORTH SCOTLAND, ORKNEY & SHETLAND

This is a place where good seafood is an assumed part of life. Go to even a small fishmonger's in a town such as Golspie in the north of Scotland and you will find fish that takes you aback with its freshness. Island communities such as Shetland and Orkney have a culture that is based around fishing, with seasonal festivals and a wide range of dialect

words revealing how important the sea is to the shore. But many fishermen here have had to leave the sea, as fishing has become increasingly unviable as a living. However, a number of both active and former fishermen have started to add value to their catch, setting up interesting smokehouses using traditional methods and marketing the likes of prepared fish dishes such as cured herring, Scandinavian style.

'THIS IS A PLACE WHERE GOOD SEAFOOD IS AN ASSUMED PART OF LIFE.'

VELVET CRAB BISQUE

ALAN CRAIGIE, CHEF-PATRON, THE CREEL, ST MARGARET'S HOPE, ORKNEY

Some of the fish arriving at Alan and Joyce Craigie's seafood restaurant, a road's width from the sea, is so ultra-fresh that it has to be left a short while to relax a touch before it is ready to prepare and cook. From a range of small suppliers they get such a variety of seafood that there might be 12 different kinds, even on a short menu of four starters and three main courses. To add an extra dimension, Alan might add some megrim, catfish or rock turbot towards the end of the cooking of this bisque. Preserving the flavour of the fish is the cornerstone of his cooking: 'It doesn't matter how good a chef you are, you cannot improve on its natural flavour,' he says. Like other seaside chefs, he rates velvet crabs as a top ingredient for a shellfish soup.

serves 4

1kg velvet crabs, live or cooked
50g butter
160g onion, peeled and chopped
160g leek, chopped
2 red peppers, deseeded and chopped
160g celery, chopped
160g carrot, chopped
5 cloves of garlic, peeled and chopped
100ml white wine
400g tinned chopped tomatoes
2 litres fish stock
50ml double cream
25g fresh parsley, chopped
salt and pepper

1 If the crabs aren't cooked, cook them by putting them into cold water, bringing it up to the boil and cooking them for 10–12 minutes on a gentle simmer. Drain and pick out the meat (see page 160).

2 Melt the butter in a large, heavy-bottomed pan and sweat the onion, leek, red pepper, celery, carrot and garlic (without colouring) until soft. Deglaze the pan with the wine, add the chopped tomato and cook slowly until well reduced.

3 Add the crab meat and fish stock, and bring to a gentle simmer. Simmer for around 1½ hours, topping up with fish stock if required.

4 Blend the bisque with a blender until smooth. Pass it through a conical strainer, pushing as much liquid as possible through with a wooden spoon, then pass through a fine strainer.

5 Put the soup in a clean pan, bring to the boil and simmer for 3–4 minutes. Add the double cream and chopped parsley, and season to taste.

HALIBUT WITH CHEESY TOPPING

NETTA HARCUS, FISHERMAN'S WIFE AND MOTHER, WESTRAY, ORKNEY

Halibut is the favourite fish of Netta's fisherman husband, Jock. Their son Iain catches halibut, as well as other white fish, on his boat The Aalskere, named after a local rock. Jock once caught a halibut that was 6 foot (5.6 metres) long. Westray is one of Orkney's larger islands (there are 70 in total; 17 are populated), and has a population of 700. As elsewhere in Scotland, many local boats have been decommissioned and numbers have fallen at the local school, where Netta works in the kitchen. There are new people coming to live on the island, but not to continue the island's tradition of fishermen—crofters.

serves 4

4 x 170g halibut steaks
75g unsalted butter
1 large onion, peeled and
    finely chopped
100g mushrooms, sliced if
    large, or whole if button

300ml dry white wine
30g plain flour
salt and freshly ground black
    pepper
150ml double cream
50g Cheddar, grated
30g fresh breadcrumbs

1 Preheat the oven to 180°C/350°F/gas mark 4. In a flameproof casserole dish or a frying pan, melt 50g butter and cook the onion and mushrooms until soft. Put them into a casserole dish if you fried them in a frying pan.

2 Lay the fish steaks on top of the mushroom and onion. Add the white wine and 150ml water. Cover and cook in the oven for 20 minutes.

3 Strain off and reserve the cooking liquid, leaving the fish and vegetables in the dish. Melt the remaining butter in a saucepan, stir in the flour and cook for 1 minute, then blend in 300ml of the strained cooking liquid. Bring to the boil, stirring all the time. Remove from heat, add the cream and season to taste. Pour over the fish and sprinkle with the cheese and breadcrumbs. Return to the oven for 10 minutes.

4 Eat the fish with tatties and peas or stir-fried vegetables.

SWEET-AND-SOUR MONKFISH

FIONA COWIE, THE HELMSDALE SMOKEHOUSE, HELMSDALE, SUTHERLAND

Fiona and her husband Alexander run a traditional smokehouse in Sutherland and one of their techniques is to use oak from old whisky barrels in their smoker. Alexander's family had fished for generations, but he stopped after 22 years to run the smokehouse, selling the family boat because it was no longer possible to make a living from it. The couple have 10 children between them, and Fiona finds this recipe a great way to get kids to eat fish. She gives this recipe in gratitude to the Fishermen's Mission for their support after the death of their three-year-old son Wallace, who was killed in a road accident. 'They help people so much, in such a quiet manner. I don't think people realize just how good they are,' she says.

serves 4

500g monkfish, skinned and
    boned
2 tbsp red Martini
1 pinch of salt
1 small egg
1 tbsp cornflour
1 tbsp plain flour
vegetable oil, for frying

for the sweet-and-sour sauce
2 tbsp soy sauce
2 tbsp red Martini
1 tbsp tomato purée
4 tbsp white wine vinegar
pinch of salt
4 tbsp caster sugar

1 Mix all the sauce ingredients together.

2 Cut the monkfish into 2.5cm cubes. Marinade it in the Martini and salt for 15 minutes.

3 Remove the fish and beat the egg into the marinade. Beat in the cornflour and flour.

4 Heat a deep pan of vegetable oil until it is hot (around 180°C/350°F, or until a cube of bread browns in around 1 minute). Dip the fish cubes into the batter and deep-fry them, in batches, in the hot oil; they should take around 40 seconds each. Drain the cooked cubes of fish on kitchen paper in an ovenproof dish and keep them warm in the oven as you go.

5 Serve with the sweet-and-sour sauce and a salad.

FISH PIE WITH DILL

SUE LAWRENCE, FOOD WRITER

'Fish pie is a versatile dish that can be served for either family supper or dinner with friends', writes Sue Lawrence. 'I like to ask my fishmonger's advice on what fish is available; a good choice is haddock, cod, hake, coley or ling. Serve with peas, or with a lemony vinaigrette-tossed salad.'

serves 4

1.1kg skinned fish fillets (e.g. fresh haddock, cod, hake, coley, ling)
450ml full-fat milk
25g fresh dill stalks and fronds
50g butter
50g plain flour
100ml dry white wine or dry sherry
3 tbsp capers
zest of 1 large unwaxed lemon
3 hardboiled eggs

for the topping
1.25kg large potatoes, peeled and halved
salt and pepper
55g butter
1 tbsp extra-virgin olive oil
25g Parmesan, freshly grated

1 Place the fish in a large saucepan with the milk. Break off the dill stalks and add these. Bring slowly to the boil, then bubble for 1 minute. Remove from the heat, cover and leave for half an hour or so.

2 Meanwhile, make the topping: boil the potato in salted water until tender, then drain thoroughly. Mash with the butter and oil, add the cheese and season to taste.

3 Strain the fish liquor over a bowl and break the fish into large chunks. Place these chunks in a large ovenproof dish.

4 In another saucepan, melt the butter, then add the flour. Cook, stirring, for 1–2 minutes, then gradually add the wine or sherry and milk, whisking constantly until smooth and thickened. Cook for 5 minutes or so. Remove from the heat and add the capers and lemon zest. Chop the dill fronds and add, then season to taste.

5 Slice the eggs and place over the fish. Tip over the sauce. Top with the mashed potato, smooth the top and fork up. Cover and chill overnight or cook straight away. (If cooking the next day, be sure to bring to room temperature before cooking.)

6 Preheat the oven to 190°C/375°F/gas mark 5. Place the fish pie on a baking tray (in case of spillage), then cook in the oven for about 1 hour, or until piping hot and golden brown and bubbling. Leave for 10 minutes before serving.

SMOKED HADDOCK BRANDADE

SUE LAWRENCE, FOOD WRITER

'You can use either regular (cold-smoked) smoked haddock fillets (or indeed whole Finnan haddock) or Arbroath smokies, but for the latter do not cook in the milk, because they have been hot-smoked and are therefore already cooked,' writes Sue Lawrence. 'Just warm the milk. This is based on Provence's dish of salt cod and potato pounded with garlic, olive oil and warm milk to make a purée to be eaten with black olives and pain de campagne.' Arbroath smokies come from East Scotland, but can be found elsewhere in Scotland.

serves 4 as a starter

500g undyed smoked haddock fillets (or 1 pair of Arbroath smokies)
200ml full-fat milk
2 bay leaves

1 large potato (about 200g, unpeeled), boiled and drained
3 cloves of garlic, peeled and crushed
2 tbsp flat-leaf parsley
juice of 1 lemon
extra-virgin olive oil
salt and pepper

1 Place the fish in a pan with the milk and bay leaves. Bring slowly to the boil. For the smokies, remove the pan from the heat the minute you see bubbles and cover. For smoked haddock, simmer for about 3 minutes, then remove and cover. Leave to stand for 10–15 minutes.

2 Flake the fish, ensuring there are neither bones nor skin, then place in a food processor. Add the well-drained potato, the garlic, parsley, lemon juice and the warm milk. Process briefly then, with the machine running, add about 5 tbsp olive oil to give a soft, creamy consistency like mashed potatoes. Check the seasoning, then turn into a bowl and cool to room temperature before serving with olives and bread.

ARBROATH SMOKIE TART WITH LOVAGE

SUE LAWRENCE, FOOD WRITER

'Arbroath smokies are one of Scotland's finest fish,' writes Sue Lawrence. 'A hot-smoked haddock, it is best eaten warm, straight off the barrel over which it was smoked, tied in pairs over a wooden pole. The smokie has recently been given PGI (Protected Geographical Indication) status, which means it must be produced within five miles of Arbroath itself, thus incorporating the nearby village of Auchmithie where the smokie was born; during the 19th century many Auchmithie residents moved to Arbroath — with their unique fish. You can also use a whole finnan haddock for this (named after the village of Findon south of Aberdeen, this is a traditionally cold-smoked haddock). Lovage is an old-fashioned herb that works perfectly with smoked fish or bacon.'

serves 4

2 small or 1 large Arbroath
   smokie
200ml full-fat milk
150ml double cream
2 large eggs
2 tbsp fresh lovage leaves,
   chopped
salt and freshly ground black
   pepper, to taste

for the pastry
200g plain flour, sifted
25g fine oatmeal
125g unsalted butter, diced
1 large egg, beaten
1 tsp olive oil (optional)

1 For the pastry, place the flour, oatmeal and butter in a food processor with a pinch of salt. Process until it looks like coarse breadcrumbs, then slowly add the beaten egg through the feeder tube. Add 1 tsp oil, if needed, then bring the pastry together with your hands and wrap in cling film. Chill for an hour or so.

2 Roll the pastry out to fit a 28cm shallow tart tin. Prick the base and chill again preferably overnight.

3 Preheat the oven to 190°C/375°F/gas mark 5. Bake the pastry blind (lined with foil and filled with baking beans) for 15 minutes, then remove the foil and beans and continue to bake for 5 minutes more. Remove and cool.

4 Flake the smokie, taking great care that there are no bones or skin. Mix the milk, cream, eggs, lovage, salt and pepper. Place the fish into the tart case and slowly pour over the filling. Bake for 30–40 minutes, or until set and tinged with golden brown. Eat warm with salad.

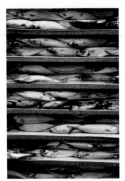

FISHING LIFE IN SHETLAND

Shetland, being as close to Bergen in Norway as it is to Aberdeen, feels as much Scandinavian as it does Scottish, and its fishing heritage is distinctive from other parts of the country.

Since the Norse occupation in the ninth century, the Shetlanders' seafaring has carried a touch of the Viking. In open boats in the same tradition as the Viking longboats, powered by six oars and known as 'sixerns', the fishermen of the late-18th to mid-19th centuries would row out to good fishing grounds, perhaps going 40 miles or further in 12 hours, bailing as they went. They would fish long and hard for cod, ling and tusk before rowing all the way back to their temporary base camps. The fishermen did this 'haaf' (ocean) fishing in the summer, after planting the crops in their crofts. They would land and salt the fish, bringing the preserved catch back at the end of the season, along with the wood used in their summertime camps. (Wood was a valuable commodity in this almost treeless place, and the wooden sixerns came from Norway.)

The seafaring nature of Shetland is evident in the popularity of the regattas and fishing competitions. Cultural traditions have also continued in the egalitarian and entrepreneurial nature of the fishing. On the whole, Shetland fishermen have long owned their boats, rather than working for an onshore owner. It is said that a Shetland skipper is essentially a part of a team, rather than a commanding boss.

In the 20th century, Shetland's fishing has become progressively concentrated on three places: Lerwick on Mainland, and the smaller islands of Burra and Whalsay. Burra is now connected to the mainland by a bridge built in 1971; Whalsay still has a ferry. A number of families on Whalsay invested in boats to catch mackerel and herring, the surface-shoaling (pelagic) oily fish. Other fishermen who didn't catch this upward spiral of investment have gradually lost the chance to fish.

As you approach Whalsay on the ferry, its harbour walls are dwarfed by the huge pelagic fishing vessels, worth £12m and more, as gleaming and glorious as ocean liners.

Inside, these boats are kitted out with the latest in fishing luxury, with white leather swivel chairs, single cabins with a TV — even a gym; it is possible to need exercise on these new, automated, computer-controlled ships. The boats pump huge quantities of fish into tanks the size of small houses.

Most of the pelagic fish caught by these boats are frozen and exported, to Japan and Africa, for example, where they are seen as useful protein. There are plans to develop more local, higher-value markets, for example by curing and marinating the fish in flavours such as juniper berry and dill.

In Shetland's kitchens it is possible to see a deeply traditional aspect to the islands' fish culture. Fishmongers sell fish heads, which are seen as good, tasty protein, and which are still used in the dish 'crappin heid' (minced fish liver boiled inside a fish head). Salt fish, the traditional way of keeping fish over time, is still part of the diet, just as it was in the days of the 'haaf' fishing. The islands continued to be far away from the main markets even after the arrival of the railways. On a big pelagic boat, for all its state-of-the-art gear and refrigerated salt-water tanks, you still see bags of salt for the crew to prepare fish the old way.

Shetland's entrepreneurial spirit meant the islanders were quick to take to salmon farming, and they are now experimenting with cod farming. As fishing declines, the new Fisheries' College at Scalloway, Mainland, is training more people for the merchant navy, with computer graphics simulating the entrance to harbours around the world — Sydney and Hong Kong, as well as Lerwick.

Lerwick no longer has the bustle it once had. A museum on the harbour stands where there used to be legions of fishing boats and the hubbub of languages and dialects of all the fishermen who flocked to these rich fishing grounds. One fishing expert said to me that he thought fishing continued here through 'determination rather than optimism'; the new roads and facilities on the islands are built on crude oil, not fish. The question is: how long will traditions continue as the fishing industry declines, as the skills and the instinctive desire for this brave, tough way of life no longer pass from father to son?

TOP, LEFT TO RIGHT A healthy supply of mackerel, a surface-shoaling (pelagic) fish, is found off the coast of North Scotland; herring, once Britain's favourite fish, is also in good supply here; a fish processing plant; the hi-tech wheelhouse of a pelagic fishing vessel. BELOW The impressive hulls of part of the pelagic fleet.

KEDGEREE

CHARLIE SIMPSON, WRITER ON FISH AND FISHING, SHETLAND

Charlie Simpson's monthly columns for Shetland Fishing News have been collected in a book – In Da Galley: sixty essays in seafood philosophy – that will appeal to anyone interested in food, fishing and Shetland dialect. A glance at the glossary tells you that pleepse means 'to simmer gently'; clatchy is 'soft and glutinous'; and booel-riving is a Viking-like description of 'hearty', literally meaning 'bowel-tearing'. The book includes regional recipes such as hairy tatties (salt fish mashed with potatoes) and crawpeen (traditionally called crappin) in which fish liver and oatmeal are cooked in a fish head. These dishes continue in Shetland even when 'needs must' is not the only maxim of diet. Charlie says this version of kedgeree, based on a recipe from the Reader's Digest Book of Farmhouse Cookery, is even tastier the next day.

serves 4

450g smoked haddock fillets
1 large onion, peeled and
    chopped
lots of butter
225g long-grain white rice
1 tsp curry paste
3–4 hardboiled eggs, roughly
    chopped
chopped fresh parsley, to
    garnish

1 Put the haddock in a large, shallow pan and cover with boiling water. Leave to 'pleepse' (simmer) over a low heat, until the fish loses its transparency; about 6 minutes. Flake the cooked fish into medium-size pieces, removing the skin and any bones.

2 While the haddock is cooking, gently cook the chopped onion in the butter until soft.

3 Stir in the rice and then add the curry paste. Add about 600ml of the water the haddock has cooked in. Cover the pot and simmer until the rice is done, inspecting every 5 minutes and adding more boiling water if necessary. All the water should have been absorbed by the rice.

4 Add the cooked, flaked fish and the chopped hardboiled eggs, and mix together gently. Serve in a dish with the chopped parsley sprinkled over it.

GARLIC PRAWNS

DAVID ROBERTSON, SKIPPER AND ONE OF THE PARTNERS OF BLYDOIT FISHSHOP, SCALLOWAY, SHETLAND

When David Robertson heard the May Day alert of one of his neighbour's boats, which was on fire, he cut loose £25,000 of gear and burst his hydraulics steaming at full speed to a life-or-death situation. The burning boat's lifeboats were incapacitated and the rescue helicopter couldn't get near because of the smoke. 'How am I going to tell the boys to jump in the black sea?' David asked. It was a rhetorical question in freezing January. They managed to get a life raft passed across to the stricken vessel and all five crew made it out alive.

David likes to eat prawns (the large ones the French call langoustines) when some of them get caught by accident in the boat's white-fish nets. At sea, he just boils them up and eats them in a Marie-Rose sauce. This dish is the one he makes for the family's Christmas dinner starter.

serves 4 as a starter

16 raw prawns (langoustine) in their shells, fresh or frozen

½ clove of garlic, peeled
40g butter, softened
freshly ground black pepper
lemon wedges, to serve

1 If using frozen prawns, let them defrost overnight in the refrigerator. Cut the prawns in half lengthways through the head. Remove the dark intestine.

2 Preheat the grill to high.

3 Crush the garlic and mash it up with the butter.

4 Smear the garlicky butter over the flesh of the halved prawns. Cook the prawns under the grill for a couple of minutes. Season with freshly ground black pepper and serve with wedges of lemon.

LING OR TUSK IN A MILD CURRY SAUCE

BO SIMMONS, COOK, BURRASTOW, SHETLAND

Ling is a tasty, good-value white fish that is highly rated by cooks in Shetland. This recipe comes from Bo Simmons, a professional cook with a passion for fresh, local produce, who for 16 years ran Burrastow House, a hotel and restaurant on the west coast of the Mainland. Shetland's history and economy are much entwined with fishing, and its presence is felt in the culture through events such as the local fishing competitions, or Eela festivals, in which ling is one of the main catches. The fish's firm texture lends itself to robust dishes such as curries and bouillabaisse. It is also salted, a preserving tradition still much in use in Shetland's cooking, and Bo uses this for dishes such as fritters. Tusk, also caught in the Eela festivals, is another underrated fish she uses in curries, or else she recommends monkfish or catfish.

serves 4

1 tbsp vegetable oil or ghee
1 onion, peeled and finely chopped
2 cloves of garlic, peeled and chopped
1 medium red chilli, deseeded and finely chopped
2 tsp ground coriander
2 tsp ground cumin
1 tsp turmeric
1 tsp ground fennel
½ tsp fenugreek seeds
3 tbsp coconut powder mixed with approximately 275ml water
4 x 200g ling or tusk pieces, skinned and boned
good handful of fresh coriander

1 Preheat the oven to 190°C/375°F/gas mark 5. In a heavy-based, ovenproof pan, heat the oil or ghee and fry the onion and garlic until soft. Add the chilli and spices. Cook for 1 minute, then add the coconut milk and simmer for 5–10 minutes.

2 Remove the pan from the top of the stove, add the fish, cover and place in the oven for 10 minutes.

3 Take the dish out of the oven and remove the fish. Keep it warm while you bubble the sauce to reduce it a little.

4 Place the fish on a warm serving plate, pour over the sauce and sprinkle with fresh coriander. Serve with accompaniments such as scented Thai rice, mango chutney, cucumber and yogurt raita, and tomato salad.

EAST SCOTLAND

The east coast of Scotland is still imbued with fishing, even though it has changed considerably since the days of local fleets. A port such as Pennan, featured in the film Local Hero, is a bank of houses all facing towards the village's former livelihood, the sea. In the 20th century, the region's fishing became more industrialized and concentrated in large ports such as Fraserburgh and Aberdeen. The oil business has attracted people to the area from

all over the world, and this has been a boom to some of the excellent fish restaurants. A number of their chefs have given recipes to this book. Fish smoking is a regional speciality, with high-class smoked haddock products, such as Arbroath smokies and finnan haddies, and smoked fish dishes, such as the soup Cullen skink, widely available. You can also visit the specialist museums, including the Scottish Fisheries Museum in Anstruther and Aberdeen Maritime Museum.

'A PORT SUCH AS PENNAN IS A BANK OF HOUSES ALL FACING TOWARDS THE VILLAGE'S FORMER LIVELIHOOD: THE SEA.'

BAKED FILLET OF HALIBUT WITH CABBAGE, SMOKED BACON AND A TARRAGON SAUCE

NICK NAIRN, CHEF AND FOOD WRITER

Nick Nairn writes: 'Halibut is widely landed in Scotland and is an absolutely topping fish – it has a beautiful texture and flavour, it's easy to fillet and the bones make good stock – no scales to get everywhere either! It has sufficient flavour to partner the robust cabbage and bacon, which is all you really need for this dish, though I'd go for rosti potatoes, too.'

serves 4

4 halibut fillets (steaks will do), 140-175g each, skinned
1 tbsp olive oil
2 rashers smoked back bacon, cut into matchsticks
1 small Savoy cabbage, quartered and finely shredded
salt and pepper
25g unsalted butter
a few drops of lemon juice
2 tbsp dry white wine
rosti potatoes, to serve (optional)

for the tarragon cream sauce:
2 shallots, peeled and sliced
4 button mushrooms, finely sliced
15g unsalted butter
1 bay leaf
3 tarragon sprigs, leaves and stalks separated
300ml white wine
300ml fish stock
150ml double cream
lemon juice

1 Preheat the oven to 230°C/450°F/gas mark 8. First make the sauce. Sweat the shallot and mushroom in butter over a low heat until they are soft. Add the bay leaf and tarragon stalks, increase the heat to full and add the white wine. Reduce until it's nearly all gone.

2 Add the fish stock and reduce until it's nearly all gone. Add the cream and bring to the boil. Sieve the sauce into a small, clean saucepan. Season, adding lemon juice to taste.

3 Heat a medium-sized saucepan. Add the olive oil and stir-fry the bacon until crisp. Add the cabbage and stir-fry it for 5–6 minutes, splashing in 3 tbsp water to help steam the cabbage, until it is tender. Season with a little salt and pepper and keep warm.

4 For the halibut, use half the butter to grease a roasting tin. Place the fillets into the tin, season with salt, pepper and lemon juice, and dot the remaining butter over the fish. Pour the wine into the pan to prevent the butter from burning. Roast in the middle of the oven for 6 minutes and place the rosti potatoes, if using, on a baking sheet at the bottom of the oven.

5 Place four good-sized piles of the cabbage combo into the centre of each plate. Chop the tarragon leaves and add to the sauce before pouring it around each pile of cabbage. Place a fillet in the centre of each plate, and finish with some rosti potatoes, if using. Spoon over the juices left in the roasting tin for extra flavour.

SPAGHETTI WITH CRAB, CHILLI, GARLIC, PARSLEY AND LEMON

NICK NAIRN, CHEF AND FOOD WRITER

'For a dish as simple as this, fresh Scottish crab is unbeatable, though you could use frozen or pasteurized crab meat,' writes Nick Nairn. 'If you go to the trouble of cooking your own crab, make sure it's as big as possible. Brown crabs are best, preferably ones that have big claws and feel heavy when you pick them up. The bigger they are, the easier it is to ferret out the delicious sweet flesh. I cook crabs in a court bouillon, or flavoured cooking liquid, as I think it improves the taste. I also cook them for a much shorter time than most people, who recommend 30 minutes or more of boiling. I love this dish with a salad of herbs on top and a glass of chilled Sancerre on the side.'

serves 4

1 live crab, weighing about 1kg, or 250g cooked brown and white crab meat

for the court bouillon
1 celery stick, roughly chopped
1 small onion, peeled and roughly chopped
1 carrot, roughly chopped
1 clove of garlic, peeled and lightly crushed
1 bay leaf
1 small bunch of fresh parsley or herb stalks

for the spaghetti
100ml olive oil
1–2 small red chillies, deseeded and very finely chopped
1 clove of garlic, peeled and finely chopped
grated zest and juice of 1 unwaxed lemon
225g spaghetti or linguine
3 tbsp chopped fresh parsley

1 Buy a live crab, then ask your fishmonger to kill it. If you cook it alive, the legs will fall off and overcook. Soon after the crab has been killed, place it in a large pan with all the court bouillon ingredients. Cover with cold water and quickly bring to the boil, simmer for 10 minutes and then turn off the heat. Leave the crab to cool completely in the cooking water. It will be just cooked, and the meat nice and moist.

2 Fish out the crab and reserve the cooking liquid. Place the crab shell-side down on a chopping board and give its back a good bash with the heel of your hand. This should open it up. Pull off the claws and bash them with the back of a heavy knife. Pick out all the meat from the claws, legs and body, including the brown meat, taking care to leave behind the feathery looking gills or 'dead man's fingers'.

3 Place the olive oil, chilli, garlic and lemon zest in a large saucepan and warm through until just simmering. Then remove from the heat and leave to stand for 10 minutes (or let it cool completely and reheat it when you're ready to serve).

4 Meanwhile, cook the spaghetti or linguine until al dente and then drain. Add the lemon juice to the olive oil and chilli mixture and season well, then add the pasta and warm through for 1–2 minutes. Add the crab meat and mix well, then the parsley, mixing again. Divide between four warm serving bowls.

ARBROATH SMOKIE FRITTATA

NICK NAIRN, CHEF AND FOOD WRITER

Arbroath smokies share the European Commission's Protected Geographic Indication (PGI) status with just a few special Scottish products, including Scotch beef, Scotch lamb, Orkney beef, Orkney lamb and Shetland lamb.

serves 4

1 pair Arbroath smokies
50g unsalted butter
4 spring onions, chopped
6–8 large eggs
2 tbsp crème fraîche or double cream (optional)
150g Mull Cheddar, grated
2 tbsp chopped fresh parsley
2 tbsp chopped fresh chives
salt and freshly ground black pepper
200g ripe cherry tomatoes, halved

1 Peel the skins off the smokies, pull the flesh off the bones and flake into large chunks. Check over for stray bones.

2 Melt half the butter in a non-stick frying pan and fry the spring onions until soft. Whisk the eggs gently with the crème fraîche or cream, if using, and stir in the cooked spring onion, half the cheese and all the herbs. Season with black pepper, but hardly any salt, as the smokies are very salty.

3 Heat the remaining butter in the pan until sizzling and pour in the egg mixture. As the mixture cooks, use a wooden spoon to gently pull the set egg away from the edge, allowing the unset mixture to flow into its place. When the egg mixture is half-set, remove from the heat and dot with the flaked fish, halved tomatoes and remaining cheese.

4 Place under a hot grill and grill for 3–5 minutes, until cooked and golden. Serve immediately, cut into wedges.

159

MUSSELS WITH A SHALLOT, THYME AND GARLIC BROTH

PETER JUKES, CHEF-PATRON, THE CELLAR, ANSTRUTHER, FIFE

This is a signature dish of a well-known seafood restaurant in the historic fishing village of Anstruther, a place that is now home to the Scottish Fisheries Museum. In 23 years of cooking here, Peter Jukes has never lost his excitement about good fish, glorying in the arrival of a huge halibut, praising the thick fillets of smoked haddock he gets from a supplier, and describing the sweetness and cleanness of the farmed Shetland mussels he puts into this dish.

serves 4

1kg mussels, scrubbed and beards removed
4 shallots, peeled and finely chopped
2 cloves of garlic, peeled and crushed
1 small carrot, cut into thin strips
1 small leek, cut into thin strips
50g unsalted butter
175ml white wine
175ml vegetable stock
50ml double cream
Maldon sea salt
freshly ground black pepper
a few sprigs of fresh thyme

1 Check over the scrubbed mussels, discarding any that are damaged or do not close when tapped. In a saucepan, gently sweat the shallot, garlic, carrot and leek in butter. Do not allow them to colour.

2 Add the cleaned mussels, white wine and vegetable stock and shake the pan. Put the lid on to steam the mussels open – this happens after a few minutes.

3 Add the double cream. Season with Maldon sea salt, pepper and sprigs of thyme. Serve after 2–3 minutes, when all the mussels should have opened – discard any that are still closed after this time.

HADDOCK FLUFF, HERBY HADDOCK

GERTIE WISEMAN, FISHING MATRIARCH, MACDUFF

Macduff is a small fishing town that is no longer the bustling place it once was, but that still has one of the few remaining wooden boatyards in Britain. It is the hometown of Gertie Wiseman, who is married to a fisherman, Albert, with two fishermen sons and two grandsons at sea. If you go to her house you are likely to find at least 10 people around the kitchen table – most of them family. When they come home from weeks at sea they gravitate here for fish suppers. These are two of her favourite recipes.

haddock fluff

serves 4

225g smoked haddock fillets
300ml full-fat milk
1 egg

50g white breadcrumbs
1 tsp chopped fresh parsley
½ tsp lemon juice
salt and freshly ground black
   pepper

1 Preheat the oven to 200°C/400°F/gas mark 6. Cook the fish in about half of the milk in a saucepan over a low heat until the fish is opaque. Flake the fish.

2 Heat the remaining milk until it is blood temperature. Separate the egg, putting the white to one side. Whisk the egg yolk into the milk. Add the flaked fish, breadcrumbs, parsley and lemon juice. Season with black pepper and salt, if necessary (the haddock is salty).

3 Whisk the egg white until it holds soft peaks. Fold in the fish mixture. Place in a greased 500ml ovenproof dish and bake for 20 minutes.

herby haddock

serves 4

4 x 170g haddock fillets
salt and freshly ground black
   pepper

25g Scottish butter
2 tbsp breadcrumbs
¼ tsp dried mixed herbs
4 tbsp grated Scottish Cheddar
250ml full-fat milk

1 Preheat the oven to 190°C/375°F/gas mark 5. Season the fish with salt and black pepper and place in greased ovenproof dish.

2 Melt the butter, then add the breadcrumbs, herbs and cheese and mix well. Place some of the mixture on top of each fillet, then pour a little milk round the fish. Bake for 15–20 minutes.

3 When cooked, you can place the fish under a hot grill to crisp up and brown the topping.

POTATO AND HERRING SALAD

MIKE SMYLIE, THE KIPPERMAN AND AUTHOR OF 'HERRING: A HISTORY OF THE SILVER DARLINGS'

'Herring for health' was a motto from a 1940s Government information film that has been adopted by one of its most passionate contemporary advocates, Mike Smylie. A naval architect, maritime historian, fisheries ethnologist, maritime archaeologist and author, Mike is also a herring smoker: hence his title 'The Kipperman'. Herring, rich in healthy omega-3 fatty acids, has been scientifically proven to be a brain food, and it can help prevent heart disease and improve immune function. Why don't we eat them more? The North Sea herring fishery was closed down in the 1970s and, while stocks have now rebuilt, the nation's appetite for 'the silver darlings' has never recovered. Processors are starting to marinate the fish to make them more convenient for the modern consumer, and this recipe uses them in this form.

serves 4

450g boiled potatoes, cooled
3–4 marinated and pickled
   herring fillets
1 small green pepper, deseeded
   and finely chopped
1 tbsp finely chopped fresh
   parsley or chives
150ml soured cream
1 tbsp lemon juice
½ tsp paprika
salt and pepper
1 lettuce

1 Cut the cooled potatoes into neat, medium-size dice and the herring into small pieces (soak the herring first in milk if it is too salty).

2 Add the chopped green pepper, herbs, soured cream, lemon juice, paprika and seasoning to taste.

3 Make lettuce cups. Heap the salad into the cups arranged in pairs. Serve with buttered brown bread or sliced cooked bacon or ham.

RISE AND FALL

The Moray Firth is an edge of Britain fringed with former fishing villages. Along this 50-mile stretch of coast, the sea used to be the life of whole communities. Today these places have ghosts; with the recent drastic downsizing of the Scottish fishing fleet, some of them are living ghosts.

Former skipper Abb Watt lives in the fishing village where he grew up, Gardenstown. Abb's shipshape front room includes remnants of his decommissioned boat, the Heisker, before it was scrapped, or 'razored' (turned into razor blades), as they say around here. His front window, like most in this village, overlooks the North Sea. It is an endless view, with a compelling vastness.

Abb was born in the neighbouring village of Crovie, with its houses washed up the steep hill like a tidemark. The family moved after a storm flooded the village, drowning five men. Crovie is now a place for holiday homes and commuters.

Growing up in a fishing community along the Moray Firth used to mean your life belonged to the sea and to God, with eight denominations even in Gardenstown. Nobody listened to the radio on a Sunday, let alone fished, and some attended three services a day on the Sabbath. Part of the fisherman's psyche is often highly superstitious, or religious. Perhaps when fate is as random as the weather, it helps to have strong beliefs.

Abb's childhood playground was the beach. The family always ate fish, often salt fish with tatties, and he first went to sea for two nights, aged eight, to catch sprats with his father, three uncles and a cousin. The men of a family tended to go to sea together, leaving the women in a state of high anxiety when bad winds brewed up.

Abb first went distant-water trawling with his cousin, steaming out 250 miles on a 30-hour trip. His first boat was called Ceol-na-mara, gaelic for 'music of the sea'. He was the mate and his father the skipper. By the time he was 21, Abb had his skipper's ticket, having studied and practised navigation and other skills.

The Heisker, named after a lighthouse on Scotland's west coast, was the summit and end of Abb's 15 years as a skipper. At 23 metres long and with 1,000 horsepower, she

was his livelihood, his home, and the place that kept him alive. On a good 10-day trip, Abb would make the £3000 a day he needed to cover his daily running costs of £1000. After these expenses were taken off, half the profit would go to the boat's owners and half would be split between the skipper and crew. A fisherman's pay depends on the catch. With the onset of regulations, Abb was only able to catch half the amount he needed to make the operation viable.

A fisherman talking about life at sea reveals a profound sense of perspective. You realise how vulnerable you are when you are at sea in a storm, says Abb. And out among the dolphins and whales, with the birds as fellow travellers, you realise that you are just in this world as a visitor. 'The best thing about going to sea is coming home,' he says. Yet, however tough fishing is, for many it is the only way of life, and to leave it is to be a beached soul.

Land between trawling trips was a brief interlude for Abb. Once the fish had been taken to market, and he had slept a bit, it was time to return. This was a life he was born to and his whole life beat to its rhythms. Why else would you do it? Abb's form of relaxation was to go freshwater fishing.

The quota system made fishing unworkable for fishermen like Abb. The catches of scarcer species of fish, such as cod, were restricted, and the over-quota fish had to be dumped at sea, dead. Of course, much of this fish was landed. After a while, with fisheries officers waiting for crews as they came in to shore, Abb started to feel like a criminal.

When Abb took the Heisker to be razored, because he could no longer make fishing pay, he took out what he wanted to keep – in particular, the wheelhouse clock that now sits in his front room – before sailing the boat to Denmark to a specialist scrapping yard. Within five minutes of docking, a flock of dealers had descended like seagulls after pickings. He flew back to Scotland.

'Fish have to be protected,' says Abb. 'But there needs to be a balance between fish and fishermen.' To find that balance requires communication between different factions: fishermen, politicians and scientists. Everyone, in the end, has a vested interest in the future of fish.

TOP, LEFT TO RIGHT **Former skipper Abb Watt; Abb's decommissioned boat the Heisker; the compass, which Abb kept when the boat was 'razored' (scrapped). BELOW Abb, who now plans to retrain to work in the oil industry, holds a picture of the Heisker at sea.**

TARTARE OF FISH

DIDIER DEJEAN, CHEF-PATRON, SILVER DARLING, ABERDEEN

The fresh sweetness of this raw fish dish is nicely set off by the silky vodka cream. Didier Dejean, the chef-patron of a top quayside seafood restaurant, Silver Darling, in Aberdeen, has seen a great broadening in tastes since he started cooking in the city in 1978, with people now enjoying a far wider range of fish and ways of preparing it, including dishes such as this tartare. He likes best of all to make this with wild sea bass. It is crucial that the fish is absolutely fresh.

serves 4

300g firm white fish (e.g. wild sea bass, halibut or turbot), boned and skinned
50g red onion, peeled
½ mango, peeled and stoned
½ papaya, peeled
3 tbsp extra-virgin olive oil
sea salt and freshly ground black pepper
2 tbsp finely chopped coriander leaves
juice of 1 lime
100ml double cream
½ tsp vodka
salad dressed with vinaigrette, to serve

1 Dice the fish into tiny cubes. Chop the red onion, mango and papaya into tiny cubes, the same size as the fish (you can use a greater quantity of one fruit, but a mixture looks better).

2 At the last minute, mix the fish with the fruit and onion, olive oil, a little sea salt and a little black pepper, the coriander leaves and lime juice. Spread a thin layer, about 5mm thick, on four plates, perhaps moulding it by putting the mixture within a ring on each plate and pressing down with the back of a spoon.

3 Beat the cream until stiff and add the vodka. Season with a little salt and pepper.

4 Serve the fish tartare with a little salad in the middle of the fish and a quenelle (shaped spoonful) of the vodka cream.

SHELLFISH RISOTTO

GEORGE SCOTT, CHEF, THE SEAFOOD RESTAURANT, ST MONANS, FIFE

This is an intense risotto using shellfish from the fine Scottish waters. George Scott, head chef of The Seafood Restaurant in St Monans, was a fisherman for 14 years. 'When I look at fish,' he says, 'I don't just see a bit of fish; I understand what went into getting it, and I look at it with more respect.'

serves 6

100g unsalted butter, diced
2 medium shallots, peeled and finely diced
300g arborio rice
1 litre hot light chicken stock
100ml reduced shellfish stock (see opposite)

12 langoustines, cooked, shelled and deveined
100g fresh crab meat, equal parts brown and white meat
50g cooked lobster meat
20g Parmesan, freshly grated
4g fresh dill, finely chopped
dressed rocket leaves and shaved Parmesan, to serve

1 Melt 50g butter in a large saucepan, add the shallot and sweat over a gentle heat until softened but not coloured. Add the rice and cook for a further 2–3 minutes, stirring all the time.

2 Add the hot chicken stock, 250ml at a time, stirring constantly; once one batch of chicken stock has been absorbed, add the next. When all the chicken stock has been added, the rice should be cooked, but still have a slight bite. If not, continue to cook, adding 250ml boiling water. Once the risotto has just a slight bite, add the hot reduced shellfish stock and reduce the heat.

3 Add the langoustines and crab and lobster meats. Stir in the Parmesan.

4 Finish the dish with 50g diced butter, stirring well to incorporate, and then add the chopped dill. The rice should still have a slight bite, but the overall texture of the dish should be quite loose.

5 Serve with dressed rocket leaves and shaved Parmesan.

SHELLFISH STOCK

GEORGE SCOTT, CHEF, THE SEAFOOD RESTAURANT, ST MONANS, FIFE

This is an intense shellfish stock that can be used in the shellfish risotto or for sauces and rich soups.

makes about 1 litre

2 medium carrots
2 celery sticks
2 medium leeks
1 medium onion, peeled
1 tbsp olive oil

2 star anise
40ml brandy
250ml white wine
1 tbsp tomato purée
3 lobster shells
50 langoustine shells
1 litre veal stock

1 Cut all the vegetables into even-size pieces. Brown the vegetables in the olive oil in a very hot pan on the stove top.

2 Add the star anise, brandy and white wine. Bring to the boil and reduce until there's almost no liquid left in the pan, just the wet vegetables.

3 Add the tomato purée, lobster shells and langoustine shells, veal stock and 1 litre of water. Simmer the stock for 1 hour, uncovered. After this, you either proceed to the next stage or you can cool the stock and let it sit in the refrigerator, covered, for a day to get even more flavour into the liquid.

4 Pass the stock through a muslin cloth or clean j-cloth. Return the stock to the stove and boil to reduce by half.

NORTHERN IRELAND

The crustacea known variously as Dublin Bay prawns, langoustines and scampi – and by fishermen mostly as 'prawns' – are one of the most important catches of Northern Irish fishing. Caught by nets, ready and waiting when the prawns crawl out of the seabed at first light, the shellfish are brought into ports and on to the market, but not before some of the fishermen in places such as Portavogie and Kilkeel have made sure

they put a few aside to enjoy at home. The recipes in this chapter show what locals do with a local catch alongside the white fish they land, such as turbot, hake and whiting. There are moves towards farming seafood such as mussels and oysters here, though there is less of a tradition of eating them than in the south of Ireland. But it is one way forward, given the decline of fishing. After all, a pint of Guinness and a dozen oysters makes life better all round.

'THE SHELLFISH ARE BROUGHT TO MARKET, BUT NOT BEFORE SOME OF THE FISHERMEN HAVE MADE SURE THEY PUT A FEW ASIDE TO ENJOY AT HOME.'

SALAD OF CRAB WITH GLOBE ARTICHOKE

RICHARD CORRIGAN, CHEF-PATRON, LINDSAY HOUSE, LONDON

'I have the fondest memories of crab from the coastal waters around Ireland,' writes Richard Corrigan. **'Boiling them in a large pot brought joy to the summer months.'**

serves 4

1 live crab (about 1.4kg)
large lemon wedge
1 bay leaf
1 clove of garlic, peeled and
   crushed
a few sprigs of fresh thyme
salt and freshly ground black
   pepper
4 medium globe artichokes

2 tbsp fresh mayonnaise
   (optional)

for the vinaigrette
6 tbsp olive oil
2 tbsp lemon juice
1 tsp Dijon mustard
2 hardboiled eggs
1 tbsp finely chopped fresh
   parsley

1 Drop the crab into a pot of boiling, salted water. Bring back to the boil and simmer for 15–20 minutes. Drain and rinse in cold water. Set aside to cool.

2 Put 1 litre water in a saucepan and squeeze in the juice of the lemon wedge. Add the squeezed wedge to the pan with the bay leaf, garlic, thyme, salt and pepper. Cut off the artichoke stalks and remove all the leaves until just the meaty hearts remain. As each artichoke heart is prepared, drop it into the pan of flavoured water (this will prevent them from turning black). Cover them with a piece of greaseproof paper and place a small plate on top to keep them submerged. Bring to the boil, then simmer for 15–20 minutes, or until tender. Remove from the heat and cool in the liquid.

3 To make the vinaigrette, whisk together the oil, lemon juice, mustard and seasoning to taste.

4 Shell the eggs and separate the yolks from the whites. Grate the yolks and whites separately.

5 Remove all the meat from the crab's body and legs (see page 160). Put all the meat in a bowl and season to taste. Lightly mix the brown and white meat together with the mayonnaise, if using.

6 Drain the artichoke hearts and scoop out the hairy choke from the centre. Slice each heart on the diagonal. Season and dress with a little vinaigrette.

7 To serve, make a pile of crab meat in the centre of each plate. Surround with the artichoke slices, leaning them against the crab meat. Add the grated egg (both yolk and white) and parsley to the remaining vinaigrette and spoon round the crab.

MACKEREL WITH SWEET POTATO AND LIME PICKLE

RICHARD CORRIGAN, CHEF-PATRON, LINDSAY HOUSE, LONDON

'Historically, mackerel is an undervalued piece of fish,' writes Richard Corrigan. 'It needs to be caught fresh, cooked, and eaten within an hour. It's great with spices to complement it.'

serves 4

4 plump fresh mackerel, filleted
unsalted butter, melted

for the spice paste
2.5cm dried tamarind
1 fresh medium red chilli, split and deseeded
2.5cm fresh ginger, chopped
6 cloves of garlic, peeled and chopped
2 tbsp cumin seeds
1 tbsp cardamom pods, seeds only
1 tbsp coriander seeds
1 star anise
1.5cm nutmeg, freshly grated
2 tsp black peppercorns
150ml vegetable oil

for the sweet potato and lime pickle
10 limes
100g caster sugar
1kg sweet potatoes, cut into 1.5cm dice
1 fresh medium red chilli, deseeded and diced
1 tbsp chopped fresh coriander leaves

for the raita
1 tsp cumin seeds
200ml Greek yoghurt
1 cucumber, peeled, deseeded and diced
lemon juice
1 heaped tbsp finely shredded mint

1 Preheat the oven to 150°C/300°F/gas mark 2. Put all the spice paste ingredients, except the oil, in a small roasting tin and warm in the oven for 3–5 minutes. Do not let the spices brown or they will taste bitter. Tip all the spices into a blender or food processor and grind to a very fine powder. Add the oil gradually to make a soft paste that will run off the spoon. Set aside (what you don't use in the recipe can be kept in the refrigerator).

2 For the pickle, peel the limes, working over a bowl so that you can catch the juice, then separate the segments, cutting between the membranes. Put the lime segments in a bowl and squeeze in all the juice from the membranes. Add the sugar and stir until dissolved. Add 2–3 tbsp spice paste. Cook the sweet potato dice in boiling, salted water for 3–5 minutes, or until just tender. Drain. While still warm, add the lime pickle and red chilli and stir to mix.

3 Before serving, warm the pickle to body-heat and stir in the coriander. To make the raita, warm the cumin seeds in a small pan until you can smell the spice; do not brown. Tip into a bowl and add the yoghurt and cucumber. Season with lemon juice, salt and pepper. Just before serving, stir in the mint.

4 To cook the mackerel, score the skin side of each fillet with three slashes. Brush the skin with melted butter, then brush on a thin coating of the spice paste. Grill, skin-side up, under a moderate heat for 2–3 minutes, or until just cooked. Serve with the warm sweet potato and lime pickle and the raita.

WILD SALMON WRAPPED IN LARDO WITH SALSIFY AND FENNEL EMULSION

RICHARD CORRIGAN, CHEF-PATRON, LINDSAY HOUSE, LONDON

Richard Corrigan writes: 'One of the great breakfast treats is a bagged salmon — ideally large steaks fried with Mum's bread. For this recipe, only wild Irish salmon should be used.'

serves 4

4 strips of very thinly sliced lardo
4 wild salmon steaks (from the centre, about 2cm thick), skinned and boned
sunflower oil

for the salsify
juice of ½ lemon
8 sticks of salsify, trimmed and halved
1–2 cloves of garlic, peeled
fresh bouquet garni of thyme and bay leaf
30g unsalted butter

for the green olive paste
8 large green olives, washed free of brine and stoned
½ clove of garlic, peeled
10 tbsp olive oil
3 sprigs of fresh tarragon, leaves only, finely chopped

for the fennel emulsion
½ bulb of fennel, chopped and feathery part reserved
1 clove of garlic, peeled and chopped
1 shallot, peeled and chopped
knob of unsalted butter
150ml vegetable stock
6 tbsp double cream

1 Wrap a lardo strip around the outside of each salmon steak and tie with a string. Cover and refrigerate.

2 For the salsify, half-fill a deep saucepan with water and add the lemon juice. Drop each stick of salsify into the acidulated water as it is prepared. Add the garlic and bouquet garni and bring to the boil. Simmer for 5–6 minutes, or until the salsify is just tender but still quite firm. Remove from the heat and leave to cool in the liquid. Drain and cut into 13–15cm matchsticks.

3 For the olive paste, pound the olives and garlic, using a mortar and pestle, to a coarse paste. Gradually mix in enough oil to loosen the paste a little, then add the chopped tarragon. Season.

4 Preheat the oven to 230°C/450°F/gas mark 8. Gently sweat the fennel, garlic and shallot in the butter until very soft. Pour in the stock and bring to the boil. Add the cream, stir, then simmer for 3 minutes. Purée the mixture, then sieve it into a clean pan. Add the chopped feathery fennel and season.

5 Put a film of sunflower oil in an ovenproof, cast-iron frying pan over a medium heat. Season the fish. When the oil is hot, sear the steaks for about 30 seconds on each side. Transfer the pan into the oven and cook for about 5 minutes.

6 Melt the butter in a frying pan and toss the salsify to reheat. Season. Reheat the fennel emulsion, if necessary. To serve, pile the salsify in the centre of each warmed plate and set a salmon steak on top. Put a small spoonful of olive paste on each steak and spoon the fennel emulsion around.

ALL PICTURES **Alex Slater, who opened The Fishermen's Mission's office in Northern Ireland, where he and his wife Trish offer support to fishermen and their families.**

THE MISSION MAN

When Alex Slater opened The Fishermen's Mission's office in Northern Ireland in 1990, it was decided that he should work from home rather than set up a Mission centre. This meant that he could move more freely, in a non-denominational capacity, around the ports, principally those of Portavogie, Ardglass and Kilkeel.

The day-to-day life of a Mission superintendent is a matter of meetings and bumping into people at the harbour; visiting fishermen's homes; quietly discovering if there is anyone in need; organising help and applying for a grant, on behalf of a fisherman or his family, from the nautical charities, then making sure the money comes and buys what is needed — perhaps a shower for a disabled seaman or an oven for a family limping along on scant funds.

Underlying the nitty-gritty of getting things done — Mission work has been described as 'Christianity with its sleeves rolled up' — is Alex's spiritual role. This part of his work becomes crucial at traumatic times in a fishing family's life. He is, for example, the man who goes to the house to tell the family a loved one has been lost at sea.

A Mission man came to Alex's own childhood home, in Peterhead, East Scotland, to inform them that his father's boat was missing. Alex's family used to go to a phone box for weekend 6p.m. calls when his father was working away. Alex remembers that day, as a five-year-old, waiting and waiting, his mother getting anxious, wondering if her husband, or she, had got the time of the call wrong. Alex has a memory frozen in his mind of how his mother was preparing supper when the Mission man came to their door shortly afterwards. In his work, he has had to make dozens of such visits: each time, because of his experience, he is keen to work with the children as well as the widow.

Alex and his wife Trish, like the other Mission couples, are there to help support the families ashore, not just the fishermen. A fisherman's wife has been described, technically, as a single-parent household, and even if her own life is not at risk, it is she who must cope with the trauma and stress inherent in their livelihood. It is not uncommon for all her sons and her husband to be together in a boat at sea when the winds whip up.

One of the women Alex and Trish work with describes waiting at the port for her son's boat to return in a gale. He had gone out because his father was ill; they needed the money to keep up payments on the vessel. 'We were never as glad as when he came in,' she says. His was the last boat to return. Another young son of hers was not so lucky; he lost his foot in an accident on the harbourside.

Alex has a range of training: as a hospital chaplain, in debt counselling and in dealing with alcohol abuse. He also has a growing understanding of post-traumatic stress disorder. Fishing is a macho business, and the general attitude to an accident is that the fisherman should go out again as soon as possible and get over it. But there are fishermen who can hardly get in a shower without flashbacks of a close escape from death when their boat sank and they were swamped by the sea. One former fisherman wakes up with nightmares of his men in the sea and the boat on fire as a result of them being torpedoed in World War II. 'Near-drownings can be swept under the carpet, but at the end of the day it comes out somehow,' says Alex. He has gently introduced the concept of counselling into fishing communities, and has made links with an expert who helped people in the aftermath of the Omagh bombing.

These are the serious sides of the Mission's work. But Alex's 38 years with the Mission have also yielded raucous tales of trawlerman antics. He and Trish raised their family in Mission centres around Britain before coming to Northern Ireland seven years ago. In Grimsby, they were in charge of a 52-bedroom centre, the nearest place some hard-core fishermen had to a home. In their stories, Alex and Trish can sound like surrogate parents of large, lawless adolescents. You need a serious sense of humour to do this job.

To work for the Mission is a 24-hour-a-day calling. The steady, sensitive work Mission superintendents and their wives do often earns them the deepest respect within the community. The quiet way they operate means many from outside perhaps do not know how important these people are: people who know, only too well, the true price of fish.

TURBOT MEUNIERE (WITH A SLIGHT TWIST)

NEIL SAVAGE, CHEF-PATRON, GRACE NEILL'S, DONAGHADEE, CO DOWN

At Grace Neill's, a Co Down pub dating back to 1611, they buy their fish directly off the Portavogie boats and don't know what they will be serving until the fish has been landed. Cod, halibut and the turbot in this recipe are generally on the menu. The slight twist in this classic recipe is the inclusion of lime juice and small capers.

serves 4

4 tbsp plain flour, to dust fish
salt and ground white pepper
4 turbot fillets (170–225g
    each), skin on

4 tbsp unsalted butter
50ml dry white wine
juice of ½ lime
2 heaped tbsp superfine capers
1 tsp chopped flat-leaf parsley
lime wedges, to serve

1 Heat a large sauté pan on a high setting. While the pan is heating, season the flour with salt and white pepper. Dust the turbot with the seasoned flour.

2 Add 2 tbsp butter to the pan and allow a few seconds for the butter to melt. Add the turbot fillets, making sure you do not overcrowd the pan. If you cannot fit all four pieces of fish in the pan, then only cook two pieces at a time. Overcrowding the pan will reduce the temperature and cause the fish to 'stew' and not colour properly.

3 Turn the fish over after about 3 minutes, cook for another 2 minutes or so, until the fish has a nice golden colour and has reached an internal temperature of around 60°C/145°F, or until firm to the touch. Remove the fish from the pan.

4 Add the remaining butter to the pan and continue to cook until the butter begins to turn slightly brown. Quickly add the white wine, lime juice, capers and parsley. Adjust the seasoning, if necessary.

5 Pour the butter sauce over the turbot and serve immediately with lime wedges, boiled new potatoes and some seasonal greens.

SATURDAY NIGHT PORTAVOGIE PRAWNS

ALAN COFFEY, SOMETHING FISHY FISH STALL, ST GEORGE'S MARKET, BELFAST

Dublin Bay prawns (also known, in places other than Ireland, as langoustine and scampi) are an expensive delicacy with a cost. In their home ports, however, they are a regular feast and eaten in some quantity. Fish seller Alan Coffey, based in the fishing port of Portavogie, cooks them up like this on Saturday nights. The quantities given feed four landlubbers; Alan doubles the quantity if feeding hungry fishermen.

serves 4

500g ready-prepared mixed vegetables (e.g. carrot batons, broccoli and cauliflower florets)
1 tbsp unsalted butter
¼ clove of garlic, peeled and crushed
40 cooked Dublin Bay prawns, shelled and with the intestine removed
300ml double cream
salt and freshly ground black pepper

1 Microwave or steam the ready-prepared vegetables.

2 Melt the butter in a frying pan. Add the garlic and let it sizzle slightly. Add the prepared prawns and cook gently in the garlic butter for 2 minutes or so.

3 Add the double cream and bring just up to the bubble. Season with salt and black pepper. Stir in the cooked vegetables.

4 Serve the cooked prawns and vegetables with rice.

AUNTIE MARY'S CHEESY FISH PIE

TRISH SLATER, WIFE OF ALEX SLATER, FISHERMEN'S MISSION SUPERINTENDENT FOR NORTHERN IRELAND

Trish Slater, wife of Alex Slater, the Mission superintendent for Northern Ireland, gave this comforting fish pie as one of her favourite recipes from a Mission cookbook. Auntie Mary is Mary Stewart, the wife of John Stewart, who worked for the Mission from 1950 until his retirement 25 years later. The recipe came originally from a traditional dish in North Scotland and it is a still a family favourite.

serves 4–5

450g pieces white fish, skinned and boned
570ml full-fat milk
50g margarine or butter
2 tbsp plain flour
salt and pepper
pinch of mustard powder
125g strong Cheddar cheese, grated
2 large potatoes (about 675g), cooked and mashed with butter and milk
2 hardboiled eggs, sliced
2 tomatoes, sliced

1 Preheat the oven to 150°C/300°F/gas mark 2. Cook the fish by poaching it gently in the milk until just translucent. Take the fish out of the milk.

2 Make the cheese sauce by melting the fat and stirring in the flour for a couple of minutes over a low heat to make a roux. Heat the milk from the fish poaching until just below the boil and whisk it gradually into the roux. Season with salt, pepper and a pinch of mustard powder. Stir in 100g of the grated cheese.

3 Flake the cooked fish into the cheese sauce. In a greased, ovenproof dish, layer up the pie as follows: a small amount of potato; half the fish in cheese sauce; the sliced hardboiled eggs; the sliced tomatoes; the other half of the fish in cheese sauce; the rest of the potato. Scatter the remaining grated cheese on top and put in the oven for 30 minutes, until golden.

PRAWNS ON WHEATEN BREAD

SHEILA MAGINNIS, FISHERMAN'S WIFE, KILKEEL, CO DOWN

In the summers before he decommissioned his boat after 32 years, Sheila's husband Frank would get up at 2a.m. every morning in order to get his nets out ready for the prawns emerging from the seabed at daybreak. This is the best time to catch them. Their son Ian decided not to become a fisherman because he saw no future in it, like many others from fishing families. (He is now a notable marine artist who paints boats with an eye trained by working alongside his father.) Sheila is one of those home bakers with a generous sense of hospitality, who bakes bread so it comes warm to the table where the guests are settled. The wholesome bread is a great partner for the silky, sweet prawns. The quantity of prawns you use, she says, depends on who you are feeding and how much you want to impress them.

serves 4

16 raw Dublin Bay prawns (or more), shell on
butter
1 lemon, sliced

for the wheaten bread
2 large handfuls of coarse wholemeal flour (about 225g)
1 large handful of plain flour (approx. 225g – it is more dense)
1 rounded tsp bicarbonate of soda
¼ tsp salt
420ml buttermilk

for the sauce
2 tbsp mayonnaise or salad cream
2 tbsp tomato ketchup
a wee 'scoot' of Worcestershire sauce

1 Cooking prawns is like cooking an egg: an extra minute makes a lot of difference. Put the whole prawns in boiling water for 2 minutes, then drain and put them into cold water to stop them cooking further. Take the tail meat out of the shell and remove the little dark intestine. Cut the meat into large chunks. Refrigerate until needed.

2 Preheat the oven to 180°C/350°F/gas mark 4. To make the bread, mix the dry ingredients together. Stir in enough buttermilk so the mixture comes clean away from the bowl (any wetter and the bread will come out too flat). Add less buttermilk than stated in the ingredients list to start off with – you can always add a bit more.

3 Toss the bread mixture gently on a floured board until it comes together. Form into an oblong shape and put it into a 1kg loaf tin. The less you work it the better. Cut a cross in the top for 'a blessing on all who eat it'.

4 Cook the wheaten bread in the oven for 35 minutes. It should come away slightly from the edge of the tin and when you tap it on the top with your fingertips it should sound hollow (or 'boast'). Cool on a wire rack.

5 Make the sauce by mixing all the ingredients together. Mix with the prawns.

6 Butter slices of wheaten bread and top with the sauce and prawns. Garnish each piece with a lemon slice, twisted up.

WHERE TO BUY AND EAT FISH

SOUTH-WEST

Alba
01736 797222
Old Lifeboat House, Wharf Road,
St Ives, Cornwall TR26 1LF
www.alba-restaurant.co.uk
Restaurant

Fruits of the Sea
01736 794979
9 Market Place, St Ives, Cornwall
TR26 1RZ
Fishmongers

Matthew Stevens and Son
01736 799392
Back Road East, St Ives, Cornwall
TR26 1NW
www.mstevensandson.uk
Fish merchants

Barclay House
01503 262929
St Martin's Road, East Looe,
Cornwall TL13 1LP
www.barclayhouse.co.uk
Hotel and restaurant

The Fish Boutique
01736 331459
Unit 14a Wharfside Shopping
Centre, Wharf Road, Penzance,
Cornwall TR18 2GA
www.wstevensonandsons.co.uk
Fishmongers

Fish Shop
01736 362982
Harbour Road, Newlyn, Cornwall
TR18 5HW
www.wstevensonandsons.co.uk
Fishmongers

W Harvey & Sons
01736 362734
The Coombe, Newlyn, Cornwall
TR18 5HF
www.wharveyandsons.co.uk
Shellfish merchants

The Pilchard Works
01736 332112
Tolcarne, Newlyn, Cornwall TR18 5QH
www.pilchardworks.co.uk
Museum and British cured pilchards

Trelawney Fish
01736 361793
78 The Strand, Newlyn, Cornwall
TR18 5HW
Fish merchants and delicatessen

Kelynack Cornish Fish
01326 241373
Unit 1d Willis Vean, Mullion,
Helston, Cornwall TR12 7DF
Fish suppliers

Padstow Seafood School
01841 532700
South Quay, Padstow, Cornwall
PL28 8BY
www.rickstein.com

Rick Stein's Café
01841 532700
10 Middle Street, Padstow,
Cornwall PL28 8EA *website as above*

St Petroc's Hotel & Bistro
01841 532700
4 New Street, Padstow, Cornwall
PL28 8EA *website as above*

The Seafood Restaurant
01841 532700
Riverside, Padstow, Cornwall
PL28 8BY *website as above*

Pengelly's
01503 262246
The Fish Market, The Quay, East
Looe, Cornwall PL13 2DB
& 01579 340777
2 The Arcade, Fore Street, Liskeard,
Cornwall PL14 3JA
Fishmongers

Pine Cottage
01872 501385
Portloe, Truro, Cornwall TR2 5RB
www.pinecottage.net *B&B*

Quayside Fish
01326 562008
The Harbourside, Porthleven,
Cornwall TR13 9JU
www.quaysidefish.co.uk
Fishmongers

Phil Bowditch
01823 253500
7 Bath Place, Taunton, Somerset
TA1 4ER
www.philbowditch.co.uk
Fishmongers

Britannia Shellfish Ltd
01548 581168
Startview, Beesands, Kingsbridge,
Devon TQ7 4BE
Fishmongers

Dan the Fish Man
07970 932566
*Dan takes his mobile fish stall
around the towns of North Devon*

The Oyster Shack
01548 810876
Milburn Orchard Farm, Stakes Hill,
Bigbury, Devon TQ7 4BE
www.oystershack.co.uk
Restaurant

**Percy's Country Hotel &
Restaurant**
01409 211236
Coombeshead Estate, Virginstow,
Devon EX21 5EA
www.percys.co.uk
Percy's also runs fish cooking courses

FishWorks
01202 487000
10 Church Street, Christchurch,
Dorset BH23 1BW
www.fishworks.co.uk
Restaurant, shop and cookery school

River Cottage HQ
www.rivercottage.net
*Fish catching and cooking classes
and events*

The Riverside Restaurant
01308 422011
West Bay, Dorset
www.riverside-restaurant.co.uk

Samways
01308 424496
9B West Bay, West Bay, Bridport,
Dorset DT6 4EN
Fishmongers

Saunders & Wilson
01305 822997
17 Chiswell, Portland, Dorset DT5 1AN
Fishmongers

FishWorks
01225 558707
6 Green Street, Bath, Bath and
North East Somerset BA1 2JY
www.fishworks.co.uk
Restaurant, shop and cookery school

FishWorks
0117 974 4433
128–30 Whiteladies Road, Bristol
BS8 2RS *website as above*

LONDON & SOUTH-EAST

Belvedere Marco Pierre White
020 7602 1238
off Abbotsbury Road, London W8 6LU
www.whitestarline.org.uk
Restaurant

Criterion
020 7930 0488
224 Piccadilly, London W1J 9HP
www.whitestarline.org.uk
Restaurant

Drones
020 7235 9555
1–3 Pont Street, London SW1X 9EJ
www.whitestarline.org.uk
Restaurant

L'Escargot, Ground Floor
020 7437 6828
48 Greek Street, London W1D 4EF
www.whitestarline.org.uk
Restaurant

L'Escargot, Picasso Room
020 7437 6828
48 Greek Street, London W1D 4EF
www.whitestarline.org.uk
Restaurant

FishWorks
020 8994 0086
6 Turnham Green Terrace, Chiswick,
London W4 1QP *website as above*

FishWorks
020 7935 9796
89 Marleybone High Street,
London W1U 4QW
Restaurant and shop

Frankie's Italian Bar and Grill
020 7590 9999
3 Yeoman's Row, London SW3 2AL

Kensington Place
020 7727 3184
199 Kensington Church Street,
London W8 7LX
www.egami.co.uk
Restaurant

The Fish Shop at Kensington Place
020 7243 6626
201a Kensington Church Street,
London W8 7LX
www.egami.co.uk

Lindsay House
020 7439 0450
21 Romilly Street, London W1D 5AF
www.lindsayhouse.co.uk
Restaurant

Mirabelle
020 7499 4636
56 Curzon Street, London W1J 8PA
www.whitestarline.org.uk
Restaurant

Quo Vadis
020 7437 9585
26–29 Dean Street, London W1D 3LL
www.whitestarline.org.uk
Restaurant

Rhodes Twenty Four
020 7877 7703
Tower 42, 25 Old Broad Street,
London EC2N 1HQ
www.rhodestwentyfour.co.uk

Sweetings
020 7248 3062
39 Queen Victoria Street, London
EC4N 4SA
Restaurant

Brian Turner Mayfair
020 7596 3444
Millennium Hotel, 44 Grosvenor
Square, London W1K 2HP

Signor Zilli
020 7734 3924
41 Dean Street, London W1D 4PX
www.zillialdo.com
Restaurant

Signor Zilli Bar
020 77341853
40 Dean Street, London W1D 4PX
website as above

Zilli Café
020 7287 9233
42–4 Brewer Street, London W1
website as above

Zilli Fish
020 7734 8649
36–40 Brewer Street, London W1 9TA
website as above

Due South
01273 821218
139 Kings Road Arches, Brighton
Beach, East Sussex BN21 2FN
www.duesouth.co.uk
Restaurant

Alan and Carol Hayes
01273 723064
201 Kings Road Arches, Brighton
Beach, East Sussex
Fishmongers

Jack and Linda Mills
197 Kings Road Arches, Brighton
Beach, East Sussex
*Fish smokers and ready-to-eat fish
on the beach*

Nigel Sayers Fish Merchants
01273 823488
198 Kings Road Arches, Brighton
Beach, East Sussex BN1 1NB

Landgate Bistro
01797 222829
5–6 Landgate, Rye, East Sussex
TN31 7LH
www.landgatebistro.co.uk

George Lillicrap
The Precinct, Ringmer, East Sussex
*Fish seller, open Tuesday and Friday
mornings only*

Rock-a-Nore Fisheries
01424 445425
3–4 Rock-a-Nore Road, Hastings,
East Sussex TN34 3DW
Fishmongers

Terry's Fisheries
01273 487268
Riverside Food Hall, Cliffe, Lewes,
East Sussex BN7 2RE

The Sportsman
01227 273370
Faversham Road, Seasalter,
Whitstable, Kent CT5 4BP
Gastropub

EAST ANGLIA

Aldeburgh Cookery School
01728 454039
84 High Street, Aldeburgh, Suffolk
IP15 5AB
www.aldeburghcookeryschool.com

Andrew Clarke
07967 209689
Staines High Street (*Wednesday*),
Kemptown (*Thursday*) Hoddeston
High Street (*Friday*)

Crystal Waters
6 Cooke Road, South Lowestoft
Industrial Estate, Suffolk NR33 7NA
*Also at markets in East Anglia and
the South-East, including Saffron
Walden, Newmarket and Crowthorne.*

John's Fish Shop
01502 724253
5 East Street, Southwold, Suffolk
IP18 6EH
Fishmongers

The Company Shed
01206 382700
129 Coast Road, West Mersea,
Colchester, Essex CO5 8PJ
Restaurant and oyster specialists

Richard and Julie Davies
01263 512727
7 Garden Street, Cromer, Norfolk
NR27 9NH
Fishmongers and crab specialists

The Fish Shop
01263 741112
5a Westgate Street, Blakeney,
Norfolk NR25 5NQ
www.westonsofblakeney.co.uk

Fruits of the Sea
01263 741721
5 Westgate Street, Blakeney,
Norfolk NR25 7NQ
Restaurant

Gurney's
01328 738967
Market Place, Burnham Market,
Norfolk PE31 8HF
Fishmongers

Morston Hall
01263 741041
Morston, nr Holt, Norfolk NR25 7AA
www.morstonhall.com
Hotel and restaurant

Norfolk Larder Fishmongers
01263 712985
35a Market Place, Holt, Norfolk
NR25 6BE

WALES

La Braseria
01792 469683
28 Wind Street, Swansea SA1 1DZ
www.labraseria.com

Coakley-Greene
01792 653416
Stall 41c, The Market, Oxford
Street, Swansea SA1 3PF
Fishmongers

Swansea market
01792 654296 (general enquiries)
Oxford Street, Swansea SA1 3PQ
Has a circle of cockle and laver stalls

The Foxhunter
01873 881101
Nantyderry, Abergavenny,
Monmouthshire NP7 9DN
Restaurant

Pav's Kitchen
01873 858100/07974439714
Merrymeet, Gwent Road, Mardy,
Abergavenny, Monmouthshire
Gourmet mobile catering van

Mermaid Seafoods Ltd
01492 878014
Unit 12-13, Builder Street,
Llandudno, Conwy LL30 1DR
Fishmongers

The Queen's Head
01492 546570
Glanwydden, Conwy LL31 9JP
Gastropub

Oneida Viviers Ltd
01646 600220
Brunel Quay, Neyland,
Pembrokeshire SA73 1PY
Crab and lobster specialists

Penclawdd Shellfish Processing Ltd
01792 851678
Unit 28, Crofty Industrial Estate,
Gower SA4 3YA
www.penclawddshellfish.co.uk

NORTH–WEST & NORTH–EAST

First Floor Café
01539 447116
Lakeland Ltd, Alexandra Buildings,
Windermere, Cumbria LA23 1BQ
www.lakelandlimited.co.uk

Furness Fish
01229 585037
Stockbridge Lane, Ulverston,
Cumbria LA12 7BG
www.morecambebayshrimps.com
Potted shrimp specialists

Mulberry Tree
01257 451400
Wrightington Bar, nr Wigan,
Lancashire WN6 9SA
Gastropub

Northcote Manor
01254 240555
Northcote Road, Langho,
Blackburn, Lancashire BB6 8BE
www.northcotemanor.com
Hotel and restaurant

Seniors
01253 393529
106 Normoss Road, Blackpool,
Lancashire FY3 8QP
www.seniorsfishexperience.com
Fish and chip shop

Southport Potted Shrimps
01704 229266
66 Station Road, Banks Village,
Southport, Lancashire PR9 8BB
www.pottedshrimp.co.uk

The Three Fishes
01254 826 888
Mitton Road, Mitton, nr Whalley,
Lancashire BB7 8PQ
www.thethreefishes.com
Gastropub

Wellgate Fisheries
01200 423511
5 Wellgate, Clitheroe, Lancashire
BB7 2DS
Fishmongers

The Star Inn
01439 770397
High Street, Harome, North
Yorkshire YO62 5JE
www.thestaratharome.co.uk
*Gastropub with rooms and deli that
sells fresh and cooked seafood*

WEST SCOTLAND & WESTERN ISLES

The Fish Market Restaurant
01687 462299
Station Road, Mallaig,
Inverness-shire PH41 4QS

Andy Race Fish Merchants Ltd
01687 462626
The Harbour, Mallaig,
Inverness-shire PH41 4PX
www.andyrace.co.uk
Fishmongers and fish smokers

Kinloch Lodge
01471 833333
Sleat, Isle of Skye IV43 8QY
www.kinloch-lodge.co.uk
Hotel and restaurant

The Three Chimneys
01470 511258
Colbost, Dunvegan, Isle of Skye
IV55 82T. www.threechimneys.co.uk
Restaurant

NORTH SCOTLAND, ORKNEY & SHETLAND

Blydoit Fish Ltd
01595 880011
Blydoit Industrial Estate, Eastvoe,
Scalloway, Shetland ZE2 0UG
Fishmongers

Da Haaf
01595 772480
North Atlantic Fisheries College, Port
Arthur, Scalloway, Shetland ZE1 0UN
www.nafc.ac.uk
Restaurant and fisheries college

J and M Fraser Fish Shop
01595 692301
Esplanade, Lerwick, Shetland ZE1 0LL

The Hand-Made Fish Company
01950 422214
Maywick, Bigton, Shetland ZE2 9JF
www.handmadefish.co.uk
Fish smokers

McNab's
01595 693893
1 & 2 Marina Business Park,
Gremista, Lerwick, Shetland ZE1 0TA
Kipper specialists

The Creel
01856 831311
Front Road, St Margaret's Hope,
South Ronaldsay, Orkney KW17 2SL
www.thecreel.co.uk
Restaurant

William Jolly
01856 872417
Scott's Road, Hatston, Kirkwall, Orkney
KW15 1GR. www.jollyfish.co.uk

The Helmsdale Smokehouse
01431 821370
1 Shore St, Helmsdale, Sutherland
(shop) 15 Golf Road, Helmsdale,
Sutherland KW8 6JN *(mail order)*

EAST SCOTLAND

Ashvale Fish Restaurant
01224 596981
42–48 Great Western Road,
Aberdeen, Aberdeenshire AB10 6PY
www.theashvale.co.uk
& 01343 552441, 11 Moss Street,
Elgin, Aberdeenshire IV30 1LU

The Silver Darling
01224 576229
Pocra Quay, North Pier, Aberdeen
AB11 5DQ. *Restaurant*

The Cellar
01333 310378
24 East Green, Anstruther, Fife KY10 3AA
Restaurant

The Seafood Restaurant
01333 730327
16 West End, St Monans, Fife KY10 2BX
www.theseafoodrestaurant.com

Granite City Fish
01738 633657
91 South Street, Perth, Perthshire
PH2 8PA
*Fishmongers. Also at Aberdeen, Forfar,
Carnoustie, Crieff & farmers' markets*

Nick Nairn Cook School
01877 389900
Porth of Menteith, Stirling FK8 3JZ
www.nairnscookschool.com

N. IRELAND

Grace Neills
028 9188 4595
33 High Street, Donaghadee,
Co Down BT21 0AH
www.graceneills.com. *Gastropub*

The Harbour Store
028 417 63789
The Nautilus Centre, Kilkeel BT34 4AX
www.a1tackle.com
Fishmongers

Something Fishy
07710 475718
Fish stall at: St George's Market,
Belfast *(Friday and Saturday)*
Magherafeld, Londonderry *(Thursday)*

CONTACTS

**Corporation of London
Billingsgate Market**
020 7987 1118; Seafood Training
School 020 75173548
Trafalgar Way, Poplar, London E14 5ST
cityoflondon.gov.uk/billingsgate
*Fish cooking courses are held at the
Seafood Training School at the market*

Invest in Fish South West
01736 333733
Barn C, Boswednan Farm,
Tremethick Cross, Penzance,
Cornwall TR20 8UA
www.investinfish.org

The Marine Conservation Society
01989 566017
Unit 3, Wolf Business Park, Alton
Road, Ross-on-Wye HR9 5NB
www.mcsuk.org; fishonline.org

Marine Stewardship Council
020 7350 4000
Unit 4, Bakery Place, 119 Altenburg
Gardens, London SW11 1JQ
www.msc.org
Info on accredited sustainable fisheries

**The Royal National Mission to
Deep Sea Fishermen**
01489 566910
Mather House, 4400 Parkway,
Solent Business Park, Whiteley,
Fareham, Hampshire PO15 7FJ
www.fishermensmission.org.uk

Sea Fish Industry Authority
0131 5583331
18 Logie Mill, Logie Green Road,
Edinburgh EH7 4HG
www.seafish.org
*Organisers of the annual October
Seafood Week*

THANKS TO...

This book, based on many people and their recipes, began with an individual: a woman who went to sea in a boat.

Camilla Sacchi has more salt in her blood than most landlubbers. During a bout of 'flu at university, she read Herman Melville's *Moby Dick,* and this awakened a passion for the sea that led her and a friend, Cath McQuade, aged 28 and 33 respectively, to talk their way on to a 10-day trawler trip in the North Sea. It is highly unusual for women to go to sea in a commercial fishing boat: there are many superstitions against it, quite apart from the fact that most people, male or female, would not have the stomach for such a trip.

Camilla had gone to Scotland with Cath to take photographs and interview fishermen for a joint project. The fishing families of East Scotland they met treated them with such warmth and hospitality that Camilla, who is half-Italian, said it was rather like coming across a northern version of the Neapolitans. It took a bit of persuading, but eventually they were allowed to experience a full fishing trip aboard the Heisker, a five-man, 23-metre trawler going 270 miles out of Fraserburgh.

Camilla and Cath mucked in, working alongside the men – gutting fish, eating softies stuffed with Dairylea and fish fry-ups and listening to Arctic tales of breaking ice on deck – always aware of the elemental beauty of the world at sea, with its ever-changing light experienced around the clock, and of the particular stamina and teamwork of fishermen working together under conditions most of us would never countenance. At four-hourly intervals there was the thunderous clang and rasp of the chains as each bag of silver emerged from the sea with the haul.

Back ashore, Camilla learned more about the way fishing communities were being affected by the decline of the fishing industry. She learned, too, of The Fishermen's Mission, and travelled around the coast interviewing their superintendents, eventually working as an assistant superintendent for the Mission in Newlyn, in Cornwall, for six months. In one stormy week of her duty, two boats went down, one with all hands.

It was to raise awareness of the Mission's work and fishermen's lives that Camilla started collecting recipes and the photographer Simon Impey visited fishing communities around the coast. It is thanks to the generosity of all those who have given recipes that this book set sail.

Hattie and Camilla would like to thank the Mission staff, contributing chefs, the fishermen, fishmongers and all those who have offered their recipes and knowledge from our shores.

Hattie's acknowledgments Many thanks to all at Mitchell Beazley for their belief in this unusual project, and their commitment to bringing it to fruition with their skills. Thanks to Diona Gregory for so carefully sorting through shoals of words and recipe instructions, and to Lawrence Morton for coordinating streams of photographs and producing such a beautiful design. Simon Impey and Peter Cassidy have done a wonderful job of bringing the taste and sight of the sea to the book. Rebecca Spry, the skipper, has kept us all going through high seas and doldrums. Thank you. My biggest thank you is to Camilla Sacchi, whose mermaid-like presence swims behind these pages. She has brought many people together for a worthwhile cause.

Camilla's acknowledgements This book would never have happened without the contributions of two people in particular: Mark Osborne, who designed the book proposal, and Simon Impey, of ebb and flow, who is responsible for the concept, for art directing the proposal, and without whose vision this book would never have been published. My thanks also to Rebecca Spry, Yasia Williams-Leedham and Lawrence Morton for making these pages happen, and especially to Hattie Ellis for embarking on this epic coastal journey, and for her sensitivity to a complex undertaking. A special thank you to Ruth, Mungo and Moya Impey for their patience; Jessica Pumphrey for affecting the introduction to bring the team together; Capt. Dan Conley and all the Mission staff; Tony Woodhams; Seb Grant; Albert and Isobel Watt; Gertie, Albert and Francis Wiseman, the crew of the Heisker: Abb Watt, Johnny Mince, James Addison, Colin French and the best female stowaway, Cath McQuade, for embarking on the original adventure.

Photography: food photography by Peter Cassidy; portraits and locations by Simon Impey except for the following, by Camilla Sacchi: 10/11, 16, 19, 20, 24, 32-3, 36-7, 38, 41, 102, 106-7, 110-11, 112-13, 135, 140-41, 146, 150 (top left), 155, 166-7, 171, 183, 184-85.

Thank you to the following publishers:

P136: extracted from *Mackerel and Creamola: stories and recipes,* Pocketbooks, by Ian Stephen, recipe by Donald Urquhart, 2001.

P165: extracted from *Herring: A History of the Silver Darlings* by Mike Smylie, 2004, ISBN: 0 7524 2988 4, reproduced with the permission of Tempus Publishing.